# Narrative
# Therapy

# Theories of Psychotherapy Series

**Theories of Psychotherapy Series**

Jon Carlson and Matt Englar-Carlson, Series Editors

# Narrative Therapy

## Stephen Madigan

American Psychological Association

Washington, DC

First Printing November 2010
Second Printing November 2011

Published by
American Psychological Association
750 First Street, NE
Washington, DC 20002
www.apa.org

To order
APA Order Department
P.O. Box 92984
Washington, DC 20090-2984
Tel: (800) 374-2721; Direct: (202) 336-5510
Fax: (202) 336-5502; TDD/TTY: (202) 336-6123
Online: www.apa.org/pubs/books/
E-mail: order@apa.org

In the U.K., Europe, Africa, and the Middle East, copies may be ordered from
American Psychological Association
3 Henrietta Street
Covent Garden, London
WC2E 8LU England

Typeset in Minion by Circle Graphics, Columbia, MD

Printer: United Book Press, Baltimore, MD
Cover Designer: Minker Design, Sarasota, FL
Cover Art: *Lily Rising*, 2005, oil and mixed media on panel in craquelure frame, by Betsy Bauer

The opinions and statements published are the responsibility of the authors, and such opinions and statements do not necessarily represent the policies of the American Psychological Association.

**Library of Congress Cataloging-in-Publication Data**

Madigan, Stephen, 1959-
  Narrative therapy / Stephen Madigan.
    p. cm. — (Theories of psychotherapy series)
  Includes bibliographical references and index.
  ISBN-13: 978-1-4338-0855-5
  ISBN-10: 1-4338-0855-2
  1. Narrative therapy. I. Title.

  RC489.S74M33 2011
  616.89'165—dc22
                                        2010030619

**British Library Cataloguing-in-Publication Data**
A CIP record is available from the British Library.

*Printed in the United States of America*
*First Edition*

To David Epston,
for brotherly care,
untamed imagination,
and earnestly discussing
every question I pestered him
with for the better
part of 2 decades.

To Michael White,
for gorgeous ideas,
a belief in my abilities,
and shouldering the weight
of our narrative community.

For all this I am thankful.

# Contents

# Series Preface

Some might argue that in the contemporary clinical practice of psychotherapy, evidence-based intervention and effective outcome have overshadowed theory in importance. Maybe. But, as the editors of this series, we don't propose to take up that controversy here. We do know that psychotherapists adopt and practice according to one theory or another because their experience, and decades of good evidence, suggests that having a sound theory of psychotherapy leads to greater therapeutic success. Still, the role of theory in the helping process can be hard to explain. This narrative about solving problems helps convey theory's importance:

> Aesop tells the fable of the sun and wind having a contest to decide who was the most powerful. From above the earth, they spotted a man walking down the street, and the wind said that he bet he could get the man's coat off. The sun agreed to the contest. The wind blew and the man held on tightly to his coat. The more the wind blew, the tighter he held. The sun said it was his turn. He put all of his energy into creating warm sunshine, and soon the man took off his coat.

What does a competition between the sun and the wind to remove a man's coat have to do with theories of psychotherapy? We think this deceptively simple story highlights the importance of theory as the precursor to any effective intervention—and hence to a favorable outcome. Without a guiding theory we might treat the symptom without understanding the role of the individual. Or we might create power conflicts with our clients and not understand that, at times, indirect means of helping (sunshine) are often as effective—if not more so—than direct ones (wind). In the absence of theory, we might lose track of the treatment rationale and instead get caught up in, for example, social correctness and not wanting to do something that looks too simple.

What exactly *is* theory? The *APA Dictionary of Psychology* defines theory as "a principle or body of interrelated principles that purports to explain or predict a number of interrelated phenomena." In psychotherapy, a theory is a set of principles used to explain human thought and behavior, including what causes people to change. In practice, a theory creates the goals of therapy and specifies how to pursue them. Haley (1997) noted that a theory of psychotherapy ought to be simple enough for the average therapist to understand, but comprehensive enough to account for a wide range of eventualities. Furthermore, a theory guides action toward successful outcomes while generating hope in both the therapist and client that recovery is possible.

Theory is the compass that allows psychotherapists to navigate the vast territory of clinical practice. In the same ways that navigational tools have been modified to adapt to advances in thinking and ever-expanding territories to explore, theories of psychotherapy have changed over time. The different schools of theories are commonly referred to as waves, the first wave being psychodynamic theories (i.e., Adlerian, psychoanalytic), the second wave learning theories (i.e., behavioral, cognitive–behavioral), the third wave humanistic theories (person-centered, gestalt, existential), the fourth wave feminist and multicultural theories, and the fifth wave postmodern and constructivist theories. In many ways, these waves represent how psychotherapy has adapted and responded to changes in psychology, society, and epistemology as well as to changes in the nature of psychotherapy itself. Psychotherapy and the theories that guide it are dynamic and responsive. The wide variety of theories is also testament to the different ways in which the same human behavior can be conceptualized (Frew & Spiegler, 2008).

It is with these two concepts in mind—the central importance of theory and the natural evolution of theoretical thinking—that we developed the Theories of Psychotherapy Series. Both of us are thoroughly fascinated by theory and the range of complex ideas that drive each model. As university faculty members who teach courses on the theories of psychotherapy, we wanted to create learning materials that not only highlight the essence of the major theories for professionals and professionals in training but also clearly bring the reader up to date on the current status of the models. Often in books on theory, the biography of the original theorist overshadows the evolution of the model. In contrast, our intent is to highlight the contemporary uses of the theories as well as their history and context.

As this project began, we faced two immediate decisions: which theories to address and who best to present them. We looked at graduate-level theories of psychotherapy courses to see which theories are being taught, and we explored popular scholarly books, articles, and conferences to determine which theories draw the most interest. We then developed a dream list of authors from among the best minds in contemporary theoretical practice. Each author is one of the leading proponents of that approach as well as a knowledgeable practitioner. We asked each author to review the core constructs of the theory, bring the theory into the modern sphere of clinical practice by looking at it through a context of evidence-based practice, and clearly illustrate how the theory looks in action.

There are 24 titles planned for the series. Each title can stand alone or can be put together with a few other titles to create materials for a course in psychotherapy theories. This option allows instructors to create a course featuring the approaches they believe are the most salient today. To support this end, APA Books has also developed a DVD for each of the approaches that demonstrates the theory in practice with a real client. Many of the DVDs show therapy over six sessions. Contact APA Books for a complete list of available DVD programs (http://www.apa.org/pubs/videos).

Narrative therapy is a truly collaborative approach to helping in which the therapist and client re-author the client's problem story. Grounded in feminist, anthropological, and multicultural theories, the narrative approach occupies theoretical space in opposition to the historical top-down approach of psychology in which dominant notions of mental health are used to explain the experiences of clients. With social justice and social change increasingly becoming part of mainstream psychological practice, narrative therapy offers an innovative and inclusive model for honoring the lived experience of clients. Dr. Stephen Madigan presents this postmodern approach clearly, with a memorable personal and narrative style. He had originally titled this book *Who Has the Storytelling Rights to the Story Being Told?*—which accurately depicts the stance of the therapist in this important approach. The narrative therapist believes there is no one objective truth, but rather multiple "truths" that provide other possible interpretations for client problems (and solutions). The narrative therapist is also acutely aware that problems are created in social, cultural, and political contexts (including the actual practice of psychotherapy) that often serve to obstruct and marginalize the very lives of those whom therapists purport to treat. This book on narrative therapy is an important addition to the series.

—Jon Carlson and Matt Englar-Carlson

## REFERENCES

Frew, J., & Spiegler, M. (2008). *Contemporary psychotherapies for a diverse world.* Boston, MA: Lahaska Press.

Haley, J. (1997). *Leaving home: The therapy of disturbed young people.* New York, NY: Routledge.

# Author Preface

During the early 1980s (when I was in my very early 20s), I found myself with a rather unusual (and particularly voracious) appetite for therapy ideas (particularly certain family therapy ideas from this era).[1] I just couldn't seem to get enough of them. Therapy's compelling storylines of hard times and human relationships pulled me in and never let go—even though my overwhelming interest in therapeutic ideas was in direct contrast to my Canadian youthful all-star hockey-playing career, which was filled with machismo, stitches, and broken bones.[2] Happily, I found a way to make peace between these worlds.

Around 1984, I was fortunate to meet the wildly inspiring Canadian psychiatrist Dr. Karl Tomm (1984a, 1984b, 1986, 1987a, 1987b, 1988) of

---

[1] I devoured the work of the Mental Research Institute (Jay Haley, Paul Watzlawick, John Weakland, etc.), Milton Erickson, R. D. Laing, Irving Goffman, and the Milan team of Boscolo, Cechin, Palazoli, and Prata. I knocked back other "favorites," like the works by the women of New York City's Ackerman Institute: Virginia Goldner, Olga Silverstein, Peggy Papp, and Peggy Penn. There were also Sal Minuchin, Lynn Hoffman, Monica McGoldrick, Murray Bowen, Harry Goolishian, Carl Whitaker, and Virginia Satir. I then crossed over a threshold toward the second-order cybernetic writings of Paul Dell, Heinz Von Forester, and Bradford Keeney (and it was Brad's book *The Aesthetics of Change* [Keeney, 1983] that helped me fall head first in love with the relational ideas of Gregory Bateson). I found myself mystified with the therapeutic feminist/social justice writings of the "Fifth Province" Irish Team of Imelda McCarthy and Nollaig Byrne and feminist hero Rachel Hare-Mustin (who wrote the first published feminist article in family therapy literature and became a mentoring friend). I also got completely wrapped up in the writings of the French/Algerian psychiatrist Franz Fanon, along with the social constructionist camp spearheaded by Ken and Mary Gergen, Rom Hare, Michael Billig, John Shotter, Erica Berman, and Ian Parker.

[2] However, when I look back, I realize the example my Irish immigrant parents (Frank and Theresa Madigan) set by working in Toronto, Canada, (without pay) alongside the poor and the dispossessed throughout their entire lives. I grew up witnessing them visit the same seniors' home every Monday evening for 35 years, set up a summer camp for underprivileged youth, work tirelessly in what were then called *soup kitchens*, make regular neighborhood visits with persons who found themselves struggling in poverty, and offer up many other generative acts of kindness.

Calgary, Alberta, who was running the (world-renowned) University of Calgary Family Therapy Program. During that time (and for decades later), Karl showed me how a therapist could stand in the hard therapeutic and political places within the field of psychotherapy. His three articles on interventive interviewing helped to kick-start my discovery and love of therapeutic questions.[3, 4]

When I first started out on this therapeutic journey, I read everything I could get my hands on. I wasn't at all certain what many of these new therapy authors were talking about, but my instincts told me that it was pretty cool stuff, and more important, the material seemed miles ahead of what I was learning in my undergraduate psychology and social work classes. I sometimes reflect on these halcyon days of reading and knowledge acquisition and realize that I spent most of the mid-1980s and early 1990s in a constant state of startled confusion and untamed excitement. However, nothing (absolutely nothing) prepared me for just how baffling my therapy journey would become in the aftermath of my first meetings with the pioneers of narrative therapy—legendary therapists David Epston and Michael White.

My personal expedition into narrative therapy began in the fall of 1986 when I attended a Michael White family therapy presentation in Calgary (this was Michael's first "official" workshop in North America).[5] He was presenting his therapeutic approach through the relational ideas of cultural anthropologist Gregory Bateson, and Karl Tomm stood beside him presenting his therapeutic ideas through the Chilean biologist Humberto Maturana.

After the workshop day concluded, Michael White walked across a crowded reception room and introduced himself to me. We talked for a

---

[3] Karl Tomm's interventive interviewing came in three distinct articles: "Part I. Strategizing as a Fourth Guideline for the Therapist"; "Part II. Reflexive Questioning as a Means to Enable Self Healing"; and "Part III. Intending to Ask Lineal, Circular, Reflexive or Strategic Questions."

[4] Karl Tomm also introduced me (and the rest of North America) to the complex relational ideas of Chilean biologists Humberto Maturana and Francesco Varela. I must have read their articles eight, 10, and 12 times over while painstakingly making detailed notes and trying desperately to make sense of all that I was reading. To this end, I even put together reading groups to help with any new or emerging therapy theory and practice ideas. Karl Tomm was instrumental in helping me get hooked on therapy.

[5] At the time of the 1986 workshop, Michael White and David Epston—the originators of the narrative approach—had not yet named their method of therapy *narrative* (this name came along in 1990, when they titled their seminal book *Narrative Means to Therapeutic Ends*).

little while about how I had managed to scrounge up the money to travel from Vancouver to the workshop and then considered all the many other alternative ways I might have better spent this money. We laughed—a lot.

Michael then inquired if I'd like to join him in the upstairs clinic to watch him interview a 10-year-old boy who was struggling with encopresis.[6] Realizing that I was by far the youngest person in the workshop and the only person wearing ripped jeans and a Neil Young T-shirt, I was somewhat shocked by his invitation, but I jumped on board.

That night I sat behind a one-way mirror and had my first experience of Michael White in therapy. I sat alongside Karl Tomm (the workshop's host) and four other therapists. Michael's practice blew my mind, and as a group we seemed quietly mesmerized by the unusual therapeutic conversation we were witnessing.

Despite all my reading and early-on practice, I had absolutely nothing to compare Michael's practice with. For example, within the first few minutes of the interview, Michael and the youngster had renamed (and externalized[7]) the problem of encopresis as "sneaky poo." White (and his colleague David Epston) observed that therapeutic progress was enhanced when the therapist and person were able to talk about the problem in a more relational and contextualized way. By not privatizing the problem of encopresis inside the boy's body, White was afforded a therapeutic space to "language" the problem as relationally distinct and separate from the child (therefore, the child's identity was not totalized as problematic). Epston and White called this relational repositioning of the problem *externalizing the problem.*

---

[6] At the other end of the therapeutic conceptual spectrum, the *DSM–IV* recognizes two subtypes: *with* constipation and overflow incontinence, and *without* constipation and overflow incontinence. In the subtype with constipation, the feces are usually poorly formed and leakage is continuous and occurs both during sleep and waking hours. In the type without constipation, the feces are usually well-formed, soiling is intermittent, and feces are usually deposited in a prominent location. This form may be associated with oppositional defiant disorder or conduct disorder, or may be the consequence of large anal insertions.

[7] *Externalizing* is a concept that was first introduced to the field of family therapy in the early 1980s by David Epston and Michael White. Initially developed from their work with children, relational externalizing has to some extent always been associated with good humor and playfulness (as well as thoughtful and careful practice). There are many ways of understanding externalizing, but perhaps it is best summed up in the phrase, "the person is not the problem, the problem is the problem." To relationally externalize a problem is not a suggestion to establish an off-the-rack description of a problem. Externalizing the problem brings forth possible redescriptions and the chance for clients to reposition themselves with the problem. Externalizing is by no means a "requirement" of narrative therapy and represents one option within a range of narrative practices.

To externalize a problem, the therapist uses poststructural accounts regarding the constituted formation of the self to relationally situate the problem and person in a correlated discursive context as a way to therapeutically externalize internalized problem discourse (Madigan, 1996).[8] For example, by using externalizing language, White coconstructed the label *sneaky poo* (in reference to the encopresis) with the young boy and personified it as a relational subject external to the child.

White then introduced a wide range of externalizing questions (Epston, 1988; Tomm, 1989; White, 1986) including: "What do you call the messy stuff that gets you into trouble? Poo?" "Have you ever had the experience of poo sneaking up on you and catching you unawares, say by popping into your pants when you were busy playing?" When the child answered *yes* to these probings, Michael went on to ask about the menacing influences that the sneaky poo had regarding discomfort, unhappiness, frustration, family trouble, and so on (White, 1986).

White also asked the family members in attendance about the relative influence the problem of sneaky poo had in their own lives. These relative influence questions included: "When your son has been tricked by sneaky poo into making a mess, what happens to you?" and "When poo stirs up disgust and frustration, what does it make you do?" Gradually (with both humor and humility), the problem's influence on the entire family was rendered partially transparent and viewed as the issue to rally around together. This manner of narrative therapy's relational inquiry had found a way to restore the family's hope and abilities.

At the time of this interview, I didn't fully comprehend the theoretical complexity and therapeutic rigor involved in externalizing problems in relational ways, but I am not sure if anyone back behind the mirror in 1986 did! However, even without a full understanding of what I was watching, I found Michael's therapeutic style of interviewing and externalizing problems highly engaging. I wanted to learn more.

Learning the craft of narrative therapy interviewing is sometimes exasperating because the structure and theory behind narrative therapy

---

[8] For some theorists of the constituted self, norms, interests, and even sexual identity are brittle constructs amenable to virtually unlimited manipulation and rapid change. As Foucault (1980) argued, the constituted self is both wholly determined and decentered.

language are not based on what is generally taught in schools of psychology, social work, and psychiatry. Narrative therapy is neither essentialist, structural, psychodynamic, systemic, nor based on individualizing principles of the self. Nor does narrative theory advocate the use of developmental models, theories of the individualized self, the use of psychological testing, or the use of texts such as the *Diagnostic and Statistical Manual of Mental Disorders (DSM;* which is not used as a basis of information or explanation in narrative therapy). Nor does the practice readily turn to pharmaceuticals.[9]

It was left up to me, a young therapist and student, to learn the basic poststructural ideas that narrative therapy was based on and its subsequent critique of psychology and psychiatry. For the most part, I engaged in this learning on my own (along with a huge amount of instruction and help from David and Michael and all the many postmodern authors I was reading).

Narrative therapy eventually hooked me by radically changing my thoughts on the culture of therapy and what life as an anti-individualist therapist could be. It was while completing my doctorate degree and dissertation on narrative therapy and poststructuralism in Florida (while at the same time training, touring, and playing in international tournaments with Canada's National Ultimate Frisbee team) that I made a purposeful decision to dedicate myself to learning and practicing narrative therapy full time. This meant hurrying up my dissertation and quitting the Canadian team (a blown anterior cruciate ligament to my right knee at the USA Nationals and a very narrative- and poststructural-friendly department chair in Dr. Ron Chenail helped my decision along).

Initially, I tried reading everything Michael White and David Epston were reading, but this proved to be quite unsuccessful given that they were studying across so many different social science disciplines and that both were incredibly voracious readers.[10] Nevertheless, I sustained my learning

---

[9] Narrative therapy does, however, view the use of pharmaceuticals as necessary for persons at certain times but does not support the widespread overuse of drugs as a primary mode of treatment.

[10] Within the folklore of narrative therapy, it is believed that David Epston read a thousand articles, whereas Michael White read one article a thousand times. This balance afforded them a certain rigor and imagination.

curve on a steady diet of exciting new authors[11]—none of whom graced the pages of mainstream psychiatry, psychology, or social work journals.

A turning point in my learning came when (for several months in 1991 and again in 1992) I was graciously invited to live and work with Michael and Cheryl White in Adelaide, South Australia (this was the beginning of a real-life therapeutic apprenticeship). And it was during these intense "home-stay" work visits that I had the privilege of fully immersing myself in the intimate particularities of Michael's narrative therapy practice and Cheryl's feminist ideas.

These apprenticeship visits also established my relationship with Alan Jenkins (in Adelaide) and introduced me to his narrative therapy work on violence, abuse, and trauma (Jenkins, 1990, 2009). I also struck up a great (and enduring) friendship with Vanessa Swan and Ian Law (who were also living in Adelaide and were Michael's first narrative therapy teaching assistants[12]).

During these same years, I was also invited to live and work alongside Taimalie Kiwi Tamasese and Charles Waldegrave and the Just Therapy Team in Wellington, New Zealand (Waldegrave, 1990). And to top off the apprenticeship, I had the great fortune to live with and work alongside the creative genius David Epston in Auckland, New Zealand, in 1991.[13] These were heady times.

To say that I took this narrative therapy apprenticeship seriously would be an understatement. For example, when observing therapy sessions with Michael White and David Epston (I would participate in anywhere from six to seven therapy sessions every day), I wrote down each and every therapeutic question in a notebook. In the evenings, I would ask

---

[11] A few of these writers included Barbara Myerhof, Victor Turner, and Clifford Geertz from cultural anthropology; I learned poststructuralism through Roland Barthes, Pierre Bourdieu, Gilles Deleuze, Jacque Derrida, Michel Foucault, and Julia Kristiva. Gayatri Spivak, bell hooks, and Edward Said were the beginning of the postcolonial writers, and I continued to follow a course of readings by Bahktin, Bruner, Gergen, Sampson, and Shotter. Then came the writings of Judith Butler on queer theory and identity and so on. I feel quite strongly that without a fellowship with these scholarly writers and areas of thought, narrative therapy practice is limited.

[12] In 1996, Ian and Vanessa moved to Vancouver to work and teach alongside us at the Vancouver School for Narrative Therapy and Yaletown Family Therapy. Our book, PRAXIS: Situating Discourse, Feminism and Politics in Narrative Therapies, emerged from this time of working together.

[13] Through these many years—and right on up to this day—David and I remain in weekly e-mail contact, passing on articles and chattering on about new ideas and narrative practice. Luxury!

Michael and David (and others) questions about all the narrative questions that they had asked that day—to get what I suppose could be called a *genealogy* of each question.[14] I would ask where certain questions came from, the intent behind their use of a collapsed and mashed up temporality (past, present, future), why a certain grammar of expression was used, what theory and author a particular question belonged to, what other questions could have been asked but were not asked, and so on.

As great teachers tend to do, David and Michael showed tremendous tolerance for my ongoing questions and desire to learn. Eventually, I began to more easily recognize a specific structure within the therapeutic interview and a particular way of positioning the temporal dimension of experience and questions,[15] and I also began to theoretically understand and phrase specific sets of words, ideas, and questions.

Every day, we saw persons struggling with a range of issues, including anorexia, night fears, violence, trauma, stealing, voices, bedwetting, and abuse. And each new session brought about new sets of questions, followed by my questions about their questions. It felt like an ethnographic narrative therapy learning lab in which no question went unanswered and no question was free from reflexive scrutiny. It was exhausting work, but slowly I got the hang of it. And inevitably, just when I thought I was finding my way in narrative therapy interviewing, Michael or David would introduce a new concept and/or author that I had to go out and investigate (to this day, I'm still investigating David Epston's leads).

Every night of my narrative therapy apprenticeship in Australia and New Zealand, and after everyone retired for the evening, I would categorize each narrative therapy question we discussed into a specific grouping. I would classify questions into relative influence questions, future possibility questions, experience of experience questions, and so on. I was fascinated with narrative therapy's unique grammar; the decentered positioning of the therapist; narrative therapy's commitment to social jus-

---

[14] Michel Foucault's concept of *genealogy* is the history of the position of the subject that traces the development of people and society (and in this case, narrative therapy questions) through history.

[15] For a brilliant description of the use of the temporal dimension in narrative therapy questions, see my 1995 interview with Michael White and David Epston on narrativetherapy.tv at http://www.therapeuticconversations.com.

tice; and how narrative therapy organized around appreciation, respect, and wonder. I would then speak each question into a tape recorder and include an annotated bibliography for each one (nerd-like, indeed).

For almost 2 decades or more to follow, Michael and David kept their generous and generative ways flowing.[16] They sent me a wide assortment of fully transcribed session transcripts (complete with additional analysis and notes), stacks of new articles to read, notes on their latest therapeutic "discoveries," interesting case anecdotes and therapeutic questions (yes, they always sent me loads and loads of new therapeutic questions).

When I returned to Vancouver, Canada (after completing my doctoral degree in the United States), I took the advice that David Epston and Cheryl and Michael White had given me about my future and resisted any and all recruitment offers to work within various institutions or universities (which at the time were many) for at least 5 years. I opened the Vancouver School for Narrative Therapy (through Yaletown Family Therapy) in March 1992. When I look back, this was a risky and hopelessly optimistic decision.[17]

As far as narrative's therapeutic history stands, my personal feeling is to view David Epston as narrative therapy's creative director and Michael White as its generative life force and unlikely (and for him a most unwanted title!) guru. Cheryl White (who founded the publication side of narrative therapy through Dulwich Centre Publications) was narrative therapy's off-the-record CEO (who kept everyone in line). The Just Therapy Team of Warihi Campbell, Taimalie Kiwi Tamasese, Flora Tuhaka, and Charles Waldegrave were narrative therapy's ethical advisors, serving us up gentle knocks on the head when we struggled with the hard issues of internalized racism, class, gender, White privilege, and so forth.

---

[16] In May 2010, Cheryl White came to Vancouver, Canada, to present at our Therapeutic Conversations 9 conference. On the last evening together, she proposed that David Epston and I spend a week in Adelaide, Australia, reviewing the 500 hr of recently found therapy tapes of Michael White (from 1982–2008). We jumped at the invitation to study Michael and his work up close again.

[17] For example, 10 days after I had (quite literally) moved into my empty office, I received a call from the local "Hollywood North" film industry wanting to meet me at my new office to discuss a therapy contract (in 2 days time). This would entail offering "therapy" to their 1,500 unionized workers. The possibility was quite thrilling (a first contract), but as I looked around the office space I realized all I had was a phone, the futon I was sleeping on, and my freshly minted PhD. I also realized that I had less than $1,000 in my bank account. So I called up a few friends, rented a truck, and loaded up *their* desks, artwork, rugs, chairs, tables, and anything else to make my Yaletown Family Therapy office look like a real therapy office. Fortunately, the meeting went well. I got the contract, and an hour later we were reloading the truck and returning the furniture to its rightful owners.

The previously mentioned unofficial narrative therapy "board" members have guided narrative therapy's worldwide international reputation and growth. They have also become my family.

## IN MEMORIAM

We lost Just Therapy Team member Flora "Mother Truth" Tuhaka on September 15, 2008. Flora had been a family therapist and a community development worker for 20 years at the Family Centre in Wellington, New Zealand. For much of that time, she led the Maori Section. Flora presented many inspired workshops at our Therapeutic Conversations conferences in Vancouver. She was a wonderful teacher, singer, and calm voice in the storm.

This book touches on the many beautiful, unconventional, and creative ideas that my good friend and teacher Michael White brought to therapy and our community. Tragically, on April 4, 2008, Michael died of sudden heart failure during a narrative therapy workshop in San Diego, California (see Madigan, 2008). He was 59 years old. Michael's wisdom plays a large part in my daily therapy sessions, and many practicing narrative therapists from around the world report this as well.

I miss him—a lot.

# How to Use This Book
# With APA Psychotherapy Videos

Each book in the Theories of Psychotherapy Series is specifically paired with a DVD that demonstrates the theory applied in actual therapy with a real client. Many DVDs feature the author of the book as the guest therapist, allowing students to see an eminent scholar and practitioner putting the theory he or she writes about into action.

The DVDs have a number of features that make them excellent tools for learning more about theoretical concepts:

- Many DVDs contain six full sessions of psychotherapy over time, giving viewers a chance to see how clients respond to the application of the theory over the course of several sessions.
- Each DVD has a brief introductory discussion recapping the basic features of the theory behind the approach demonstrated. This allows viewers to review the key aspects of the approach about which they have just read.
- DVDs feature actual clients in unedited psychotherapy sessions. This provides a unique opportunity to get a sense of the look and feel of real psychotherapy, something that written case examples and transcripts sometimes cannot convey.
- There is a therapist commentary track that viewers may choose to play during the psychotherapy sessions. This track gives unique insight into why therapists do what they do in a session. Further it provides an in

vivo opportunity to see how the therapist uses the model to conceptualize the client.

The books and DVDs together make a powerful teaching tool for showing how theoretical principles affect practice. In the case of this book, the DVD *Narrative Therapy Over Time,* which features the author as the guest expert, provides a vivid example of how this approach looks in practice.

# Acknowledgments

People's life stories have shaped this book—thousands of them. I embrace these stories with respect and appreciation. To all you insider interlocutors I say thank you for trust, teaching, and transparency:

Taimalie Kiwi Tamasese and Charles Waldegrave, for loyal friendship and fierce ideas;

Cheryl White, for shaping me more than she knows;

Karl Tomm, for integrity and grit that I respect immensely;

Heather Elliot and Colin Sanders, for radical practice passion and patching together The Vancouver School for Narrative Therapy;

Vicki Dickerson, Bill Lax, and Jeff Zimmerman, for highly entertaining early narrative years;

Imelda McCarthy and Nolliag Byrne, for Irish sensibility and deft theoretical ethics;

Narrative therapy colleagues around the world, for years of ongoing laughter, new ideas, and hope;

Jon Carlson, for zen living and inviting me onto yet another one of his marvelous projects;

James Justice Partlow, for pursuing justice when it mattered most;

David Denborough, for an exceptionally cool and quick edit on this book after it exceeded the contracted page limit;

My parents, Frank and Theresa Madigan, for their tireless work with the poor and dispossessed and showing me social justice, a class analysis, and the meaning behind a labor of love;

The women in my life—Anne, Mary, Hannah, Tessa, Mara, Maresa, Robin, Hilda, Elizabeth, Gail, Vikki, Brenda, and Danielle—for loving care, a sense of wonder, and showing me how the feminist sisterhood works; and

The brothers—Paul, Andrew, Patrick, Elliot, Les, Martin, Vincent, Ian, David, Darryl, and Colin—for love in the hard times and smart-mouthing authority ever since we were kids.

# Narrative Therapy

# 1

# Introduction

*Whatever sense we have of how things stand with someone else's inner life,*
*we gain it through their expressions, not through some magical intrusion*
*into their consciousness. It's all a matter of scratching surfaces.*

(Geertz, 1988, p. 373)

This book intends to unlock the mysteries of narrative therapy theory and practice by escorting the reader on a casual intellectual stroll through narrative therapy's personal, theoretical, and practice history. Australian therapist Michael White and Canadian cum New Zealand immigrant David Epston began their novel therapeutic work in the early 1980s but did not coin the term *narrative therapy* until 1989. By the early 1990s, their ideas had a relatively small but passionate following throughout North American and Europe. In 2010–2011, narrative therapy is at the theoretical center of how thousands of therapists practice worldwide.

Renowned American cultural anthropologist Clifford Geertz (1976) wrote that

> the Western conception of the person as a bounded, unique, more or
> less integrated motivational and cognitive universe, a dynamic centre

of awareness, emotion, judgment, and action organized into a distinctive whole and set contrastively against a social and natural background is, however incorrigible it may seem to us, a rather peculiar idea within the context of the world's cultures. (p. 229)

Geertz (1973, 1976, 1983) described a view of human identity that is considered relational, contextual, communal, discursive, and anti-individualist. Narrative therapy holds this same point of view. At the heart of David Epston and Michael White's practice in narrative therapy is an unswerving commitment to a relational/contextual/anti-individualist[1] therapeutic view of people and relationships. This relational/contextual/anti-individualist practice was founded on a therapy designed to counter psychologies idea of the skin-bound individual self.

Epston and White's narrative therapy contends that to properly study a "self," a reader must understand how it is related to his or her own personal concept of self (Madigan, 2004, 2007).[2,3] A narrative therapy point of view brings forth a multisited and multistoried idea of the subject.[4] Narrative therapy's approach to the self stretches out beyond the more popu-

---

[1] During a conversation in Vancouver, Canada, in October 2009, David Epston stated that more than anything else, he and Michael White had organized their therapeutic work through an anti-individualist/prorelational theory and practice.

[2] This discursive self-perception plays a critical role in one's interpretation of meaning. Whereas different poststructural thinkers' views on the self vary, the self under study is said to be constituted by discourse(s) (Foucault, 1979).

[3] For example, in a poststructural approach to textual analysis, it is the reader of a text that replaces the author as the primary subject of inquiry. This displacement is often referred to as the *destabilizing* or *decentering* of the author (in our case, think of the therapist), although it has its greatest effect on the text itself (Derrida, 1991).

[4] In an unpublished interview, Michael White responded to a question regarding the limits of systems thinking by suggesting that when considering systems thinking, one needs a close-up review of the effects of modernist notions of the self; structuralism; science; individualizing problems; ethnocentric/eurocentric White beliefs; dominant ideas of race, gender, sexual preference; family values; Parsonian ideas; and so on. He also suggested that the problem with this mode of thinking is that many well-intentioned therapy practices have cloned themselves onto ideas that have, for the most part, remained unchallenged (some would say "taken for granted ideas") and look at the movement from first-order and second-order systems thinking, both of which are structural in their intent and practice; however, it could be stated that most therapy practice is of the first order (even though Bateson's thinking spawned a great excitement). Let's not forget that systems thinking was brought to light within Bowenian family of origin, Minuchin's structural therapy and the Medical Research Institute's strategic thinking, and Milan's circularity and hypothesizing (these therapies are often put together in a hurly-burly mixture and represent the popular therapeutic practice brands, and these traditions have already been deconstructed from many points of view, but the practice carries on—the question is, Why?). Therapists have argued for decades from the position that if systems thinking is so outdated, how come so many "clients" have been helped in the process? This, of course, is not the point.

lar and/or generalized accounts of who persons are (e.g., dominant and/or individualized categories of personhood) and of who the person is stated or labeled to be by the expert of psychological knowledge (Madigan, 1997).

I received a call from a staff person at a local psychiatric ward asking if I would consider counseling Tom. Tom was described to me as "suicidal and depressed," a person on whom the hospital had "tried everything possible." The "everything" they had tried included 40 electroconvulsive therapy (ECT) sessions within a 12-month period, six varieties of selective serotonin reuptake inhibitors and antipsychotic medication within a 12-month period, and a year's worth of group and individual cognitive–behavioral talk therapy.

The hospital staff person explained that the therapy staff had "all but given up" on Tom—a 66-year-old White, middle-class, able-bodied, married, heterosexual male. They said that Tom had been living "off and on" (more on than off) as an "unsuccessful patient" within the hospital institution for just over a year. And although he had been administered a variety of psychiatric technologies of normalization in various forms, "nothing had worked."

Throughout the 12 months of hospital contact, Tom had participated in the hospital's ongoing systematic creation, classification, and control of anomalies in his social body. From my discussions with the hospital staff (who had worked alongside Tom throughout the year), Tom's "chronic" body had been attributed and situated within particular sets of psychological meaning (i.e., a severely depressed person). This helped lead me to imagine that Tom's body had fit categorically within the memorized moments of psychological history—read through the archives of certain expert others—and then transformed into professional documents regarding who in fact Tom was.

When I first met Tom, he weighed in with a 6-pound hospital case file. From where I was standing on the outside, it looked to me like Tom had been unanimously described as a chronic major depressive disorder. This suggested that the documented Tom (or the Tom of-the-file) was viewed by the staff within the confines of an essentialist, interior (modern) self. Our phone conversations, as well as the hospital's interpretations of Tom, translated through the case files, helped me locate the context of the staff's expertise of knowledge[5] about Tom.

The obvious contradiction in my contact with the hospital was realizing that the hospital had condemned Tom to a life of (chronic) identity death (in that *chronic* means he could not be helped; Madigan, 1999); at the same time, the hospital desired him to "recover" through their psychiatric technology. Unfortunately, Tom was judged to be unfit because he could not please the hospital team (primarily because their psychological practices did not work for him). And as the hospital staff's limited description might suggest, Tom became both cultural object and intellectual product of the institution (Madigan, 1996).

Within the model of scientific medicine and understanding that the psychiatric ward used to situate Tom, the body of the subject (in this case the body of Tom) was viewed as the passive tablet on which (his or her) disorders were inscribed (written onto). In other words, the hospital staff's knowledge was used to write pathologies onto and about Tom's body. Deciphering the proper inscription to fit with Tom's body was a matter of determining a cause of the disorder and required an interpretation of the symptoms fitting within their prevailing diagnostic texts.[6]

The process of Tom being inscribed into the *Diagnostic and Statistical Manual of Mental Disorders* (*DSM*) text required a trained (i.e., highly specialized) professional who was afforded the opportunity and privilege to unlock the secrets of Tom's disordered body. This specialized knowledge, mediated through specific sets of agreed-on power relations and those subsequent levels of professional status afforded (to us professionals), allowed a hospital professional to bring this forward as a meaningful description of Tom.

---

[5] Michael White (1995a) wrote that "since the pathologizing discourses are cloaked in impressive language that establishes claims to an objective reality, these discourses make it possible for mental health professionals to avoid facing the real effects of, or the consequences of, these ways of speaking about and acting towards those people who consult them. If our work has to do with subjecting person's to the 'truth', then this renders invisible to us the consequences of how we speak to people about their lives, and of how we structure out interactions with them; this mantle of 'truth' makes it possible for us to avoid reflecting on the implications of our constructions and of our therapeutic interactions in regard to the shaping of people's lives" (p. 115).

[6] With over 400 possible ways to be considered abnormal (Breggin, 1994; Caplan, 1995), plotting a person's entire life story within the text of the *DSM* is not that uncommon or difficult (for some) to achieve.

These abilities and story-naming rights are negotiated and distributed through the professional institution and its archives (Foucault, 1972). This naming procedure dictates the control of who gets to say what about who is normal and who is not, and what will be done as a consequence and with what authority (Madigan, 1997). Central to the narrative therapy critique of the modernist psychological platform (which includes a critique of *DSM* technology[7]) is the analysis of who should not be afforded legitimate speaking rights because they have not acquired the proper rational inquiry brought on as a result of systematic thought and orderly investigation (Madigan, 2008).

Tom, for our purposes now known as the *person without knowledge* (Madigan, 2003), was viewed as operating without a context (thereby he was viewed to live in a disembodied context) but classified within gender, race, age, ability, sexual orientation, and "dysfunction." It appears from my contact with the hospital staff that Tom could only acquire legitimized speaking rights through a specified institutional matrix that distributes and negotiates (in this case psychological/psychiatric) knowledge, power, and his storytelling rights.

After my contact with the hospital professionals, I saw Tom in therapy for eight sessions over the course of 3 months. He left the hospital ward after the fifth session during Week 7 and never returned. His speech continued to be a little bit slurred because of the numerous ECT sessions, but overall he and his family members reported that his comeback had been quite successful. Our conversations concentrated on separating Tom from the totalized chronic identity description of major depression that had been wrongly applied to him and on helping him remember aspects and abilities of his life that the problem's identity conclusions had helped him remember to forget.

During our eight sessions of narrative therapy, there were no other-worldly charms or scientific medicines used in helping Tom get his life back from depression. Quite simply (as I reported back to the hospital

---

[7]One (of the many) differences narrative therapy has with the *DSM–IV* manual is that it has no consistent requirement that the everyday behavior used as diagnostic criteria actually be the result of mental disorder and not the result of other life experiences (Crowe, 2000).

staff), Tom had stated plainly that he had experienced a lot of appreciation, compassion, and listening during our talks and through the influx of therapeutic letters from his community of concern. He also stated that he liked the way we stepped "outside the box" to get a better understanding of his relationship with the problem and how we reviewed aspects and stories of his life that could not be explained through the problem and the hospital's definition of him.

Tom (under the supervision of a medical doctor) committed to get off all the psychiatric medications prescribed to him by Week 12 of our therapy. By Week 12 he was also volunteering at an AIDS hospice, gardening a few vegetable plots, and having "a lot of fun" with his grandchildren. Tom had also became an antidepression consultant to the Vancouver School for Narrative Therapy's year-long narrative therapy program.

For the first-time reader, entering into the theoretical ideas raised in this book (and their application to therapy) can be a difficult and a somewhat daunting task. However, the book makes every attempt to rescue the reader from as much discomfort as possible by deciphering the intellectual rigor and code of the poststructural theory/narrative therapy relationship and by placing the theory alongside the imagination of common everyday narrative therapy practice examples.

Throughout the book's theoretical discussion, I show that unlike the formal systems of psychological analysis, narrative therapy does not seek to establish global accounts of life and universal categories of human nature by constructing naturalized and essentialist notions of the self (Madigan, 1992, 1996, 2008). Narrative therapy finds no cause or reason to diagnose and/or label a person's lived experience.

David Epston and Michael White perceived that all formal diagnostic analysis produced flat monologic[8] descriptions of psychological life that attempt to render events predictable (J. Bruner, 1986; Parker, 2008; Sampson, 1993). They found that psychology's more formalized description of personhood championed the norm through generalizations regarding who

---

[8] Conventional psychological thinking supporting the idea of a self-contained individual who is fundamentally monologic: "a hermetic and self-sufficient whole, one whose elements constitute a closed system presuming nothing beyond themselves, no other utterances" (Bakhtin, 1981, p. 273).

people actually were, whereas narrative metaphors were based in a dialogic encounter—rendering the unexpected invisible and unique, so as not to be misled by the general (M. White, personal communication, 1992[9]).

This book on narrative therapy explores several key poststructural concepts that provide a foundation for narrative therapy practice. These concern the relationship between power and knowledge, structural inequalities, the textual identity of the dialogic person, the social location of the multisited person, the influence prevailing cultural discourse has on the shaping of how we view persons and problems, and questions on the origin and location of problems.

By way of numerous case examples, the book demonstrates how poststructural theory finds a congruent fit within a practice of narrative therapy. The book also explores how the primary objective of narrative therapy interviewing is to demystify deviations in the problem story being told.

The book highlights a few key questions pertinent to the construction of narrative therapy practice regarding (a) what gets to be said in therapy (e.g., about persons and problems and within other institutions like medicine, the judiciary, psychiatric wards, school systems, families, media) regarding a person's identity and problems, (b) who gets to say what about people and problems in therapy, and (c) with what professional influence. The exploration of these particular therapeutic questions, as well as the formation of the questions themselves, is shaped by poststructural theory throughout.

Finally, the primary question I attempt to raise in the book is based on a rather simple question: Who has the storytelling rights to the story being told?

---

[9] Throughout the book, I will be referring to particular personal conversations I have had with people who influenced my work. These dialogues were part of an ever-growing fabric of up-close conversational learning and are not necessarily found in books or articles. To see some of these public dialogues on a wide range of topics, go to The History of Change Interviews on narrativetherapy.tv (http://therapeuticconversations.com/?page_id=60).

# 2

# History

*A critique does not consist in saying that things aren't good the way they are.*
*It consists in seeing on just what type of assumptions, of familiar notions, of*
*established and unexamined ways of thinking the accepted practices are based.*
*To do criticism is to make harder those acts which are now too easy.*

—Michel Foucault

Much has been written about the "magic," "difference," and "mystique" of Epston and White's practice of narrative therapy.[1] I imagine that what made their narrative therapy practice different from what had preceded them was their decision to embrace the enormous body of scholarship directed toward uncovering the ideological, political, and ethical biases underlying the authority for psychological knowledge.

---

Portions of this chapter have been excerpted or adapted from handouts created by Stephen Madigan for use in his workshops at the Therapeutic Conversations conferences.

[1] The term *narrative therapy* has a specific meaning and is not the same as narrative psychology or any other therapy that uses stories. Narrative therapy refers to the ideas and practices of David Epston and Michael White (along with the many contributions their international colleagues throughout the world have made).

For their theoretical inspiration, White and Epston turned away from prevailing psychological, psychiatric, systemic, and all other theoretical and practice views informed by individualism. Instead, they moved their therapy practice toward specific poststructural theories that informed ideas regarding a relational identity. They found these ideas situated within the disciplines of cultural anthropology, feminism, postcolonialism, anti-oppression, social justice, literary theory, and queer studies (to name just a few of the disciplines). In addition, they were influenced by the leading voices of French poststructural philosophy (circa 1965 to the present).

White and Epston's philosophical turn away from psychological theory and practice, along with their deft ability to translate the "high" disciplines of poststructural theory into a helpful day-to-day practice of therapy, thrust this unlikely pair onto the world stage and toward international notoriety.[2] McLeod (1997) went so far as to categorize narrative therapy as the field's first (and perhaps only) postpsychological[3] therapy.

From the beginning, a central poststructural[4] tenet of narrative therapy was the idea that we, as persons, are "multistoried" (J. Bruner, 1990; Geertz, 1973, 1983). Simply stated, narrative therapists took up the position that within the context of therapy, there could be numerous interpretations

---

[2] Academics and therapists always seem surprised when they find out that Epston's background is "only" a master's degree in social work and White merely held a bachelor's degree of social work.

[3] *Postpsychological* refers to a practice of therapy ideas that has questioned the underpinnings of psychological knowledge and practice and moved beyond psychology's foundational ideological/theoretical and practice tenets.

[4] A definition of poststructuralism can be found at http://www.philosopher.org.uk/poststr.htm: "By the mid-20th century, there were a number of structural theories of human existence. In the study of language, the structural linguistics of Ferdinand de Saussure (1857–1913) suggested that meaning was to be found within the structure of a whole language rather than in the analysis of individual words. For Marxists, the truth of human existence could be understood by an analysis of economic structures. Psychoanalysts attempted to describe the structure of the psyche in terms of an unconscious. In the 1960s, the structuralist movement based in France attempted to synthesize the ideas of Marx, Freud, and Saussure. Members of the movement disagreed with the existentialists' claim that each person is what he or she makes of himself or herself. For the structuralist, the individual is shaped by sociological, psychological, and linguistic structures over which he or she has no control but that could be uncovered by using their methods of investigation. Originally labeled a structuralist, the French philosopher and historian Michel Foucault came to be seen as the most important representative of the poststructuralist movement. He agreed that language and society were shaped by rules and governed systems, but he disagreed with the structuralists on two counts. First, he did not think that there were definite, underlying structures that could explain the human condition, and second, he thought that it was impossible to step outside of discourse and survey the situation objectively. Jacques Derrida (1930–2004) developed deconstruction as a technique for uncovering the multiple interpretation of texts. Influenced by Heidegger and Nietzsche, Derrida suggested that all text has ambiguity, and because of this, the possibility of a final and complete interpretation is impossible."

about persons and problems (Geertz, 1976; Myerhoff, 1982, 1986). And the very interpretations (of persons and problems) that therapists bring forward are mediated through prevailing ideas held by our culture regarding the specifics of who and what these persons and problems are and what they represent (e.g., normal/abnormal, good/bad, worthy/unworthy).

In Michael White's (1989) *Selected Papers* (his writings from 1978–1988) and David Epston's (1988) *Collected Papers* (from 1983–1988), the sharp ingenuity of their practice is readily apparent.[5] Their earliest published work through Dulwich Centre Publications in Adelaide, South Australia, introduced the reader to a plethora of fresh ideas on new approaches to long-standing problems, therapeutic letter writing, rites of passage, unique outcomes, relative influence questions, therapeutic documents, externalizing conversations, alternative/subordinate stories, and a wide variety of curiosities and inquiries—all designed and communicated through narrative questions and letter writing and originating from a new form of therapeutic grammar (White & Epston, 1990).

Epston has stated that during the 1980s he was most affected by ideas in relation to definitional ceremony and a lively debate in cultural anthropology (Geertz, 1973; Myerhoff, 1992; Turner, 1986; Tyler, 1986) involving the problems in representation in writing (D. Epston, personal communication, 1991). David was fascinated with how therapy could use the ideas of blurred genres and literary process by using metaphor and narrative to affect the many ways in which phenomena are registered from the first observations, to the completed book, to the ways these configurations made sense in determining acts of reading (Epston, 1988, p. 7). He decided early on to forgo the "distancing rhetoric" required in scientific "writing up" and chose instead to use his own (and the person's) ethnographic voice as a way to pervade and situate the person's own unique accounting of events.

A few of Epston's (1988) remarkable writings from this period stand out for me, such as "The Story of Dory the Cat," "Short Stories on School

---

[5] Both David Epston and Michael White began their therapeutic work with children. And many years before their practice was called *narrative therapy*, they were both externalizing problems with the children they were working with. Despite the fact that each of them was working with some terrifying childhood problems, their practice of therapy was always playful, engaging, sometimes hilarious, and always rigorously accountable.

Refusing," "Counter-Dreaming," "Are You a Candidate for Mental Karate?" (coauthored with "Ben"), and "Tiger Taming." These early published examples demonstrate how his therapeutic practice was not only (regularly) wholly inventing new ways of working with specific problems but at the same time creating a new line of language and thought to accompany these novel therapeutic performances.

Observing David Epston work in therapy up close is breathtaking. The first time (in 1991) that I witnessed his therapy "live," I felt like I was watching an art form more in line with John Coltrane or Picasso. When reading David's work, one realizes that he was continually inventing and generating new therapeutic practice ideas. His creativity seemed to stem from his first realization that ongoing behavioral and structural approaches to treating problems encountered by children and adults were largely ineffective. And rather than complain that an approach wasn't working (which is what we usually tend to do in therapy), he took up the challenge to turn a noneffective therapy into a newly formed method for problem resolution.[6]

Epston invented new therapy methods by using his talent for spotting and then undermining the life support systems of problems (those that are often supported through the very practices of therapy[7]). He then found new therapeutic practices to counter them. He did this through his unwavering belief in close-up ethnographic interviewing with the people he works with. He transported the insider's problem knowledge into new ways of working differently with many hard-to-resolve issues. As a result, David was responsible for introducing the novel practice of therapeutic letter writing and many other practices of the written word into the field of narrative therapy.[8]

Early on in his therapeutic practice, Epston seemed to make it his mission to work against any form of therapy that acted as a ritual of degradation—in

---

[6] For example, to put his extraordinary therapeutic work into some kind of perspective, I realized that when Epston first wrote "The Case of the Night Watchman" (1988; originally conceived of in 1979), he had virtually invented an entirely new genre of therapeutic work with children. This can also be said of his work with couples as well as individuals with eating disorders, anxiety, worry, asthma, and more.

[7] Please refer to Helen Gremillion's book *Feeding Anorexia* for an excellent example of how well-meaning institutional systems often help problems grow larger.

[8] When I went to study and live with David in Auckland during spring 1991, he had already penned thousands of therapeutic letters—writing letters to clients at the end of every session.

which one party (i.e., the professional helper) would act to make the other party feel "less than." For Epston, taken-for-granted assumptions of everyday life became a focus of inquiry and celebration.

In his writings, he appears to have single-mindedly committed to transforming what was normally taken as pathology into descriptions of valor, intrigue, and courage (D. Epston, personal communication, 1993). He incorporated the importance of anthropology's idea of ritualization and rites of passage (Geertz, 1983; Myerhoff, 1982), and he brought these ideas into the center of his work by highlighting a reincorporation phase to therapy. He promoted this concept by encouraging celebrations, awards, diplomas, and parties to commemorate a person's achievements of undermining long-standing problems (Epston, 1988; White, 1988/1989).

Meanwhile, Michael White was working out new forms of practice with children who were struggling with encopresis—in 90-degree Australian heat—in an unventilated therapy room located in the basement of a local Adelaide hospital. His therapy work was first "discovered" by North American and European therapists through an article he wrote in 1984 entitled "Pseudo-Encopresis: From Avalanche to Victory, From Vicious to Virtuous Cycles."[9] It was during this period of his career that he was most interested in cybernetic theory and, more specifically, in Gregory Bateson's (1972, 1979) ideas of negative explanation, restraint, and news of information and difference.

Throughout my apprenticeship in narrative therapy, I found that to move toward a fuller understanding of Michael White's therapeutic thinking, it was important to first figure out his relationship to Gregory Bateson (Bateson, 1972, 1979). For example, White organized his early conceptual and practice work of externalizing conversations through Bateson's notions of restraint, difference, and double description[10] (M. White, personal communication, 1991).

---

[9] White published his first article in 1979 in the journal *Family Process*. It is titled "Structural and Strategic Approaches to Psychodynamic Families."

[10] Munro (1987, p. 185) wrote that double description challenges restraints, thus triggering new solutions; for example, the second description and the new perceptions of this description allow the client to experience a view of the problem (and of themselves) that is not bound by the restraints under their first description operated.

Briefly, Bateson's thinking about restraints was as follows: that events, persons, ideas, and so on, travel their course of action not because they have to (or are born to) but because they are restrained from taking any other course of action (Bateson, 1979). White (1988/1989) interpreted Bateson's ideas this way:

> Restraints take various forms and include the network of presupposi-
> tions, premises, and expectations that make up the family members
> map of the world, and that establishes rules for the selection of infor-
> mation about perceived objects or events, thus contributing to sensory
> limitations. (p. 85)

Bateson's theoretical position of restraints led White to state that any therapeutic story about a person that did not involve a theory of restraints would usually end up being a statement that pathologized the person/family/couple/group (M. White, personal communication, 1990).

By comparison, a more traditional intrapsychic perspective on, for example, child sexual assault views the client as owning a pathology, which the therapist expert on pathology will fix through "accurate diagnosis" and "treatment" (Justice & Justice, 1979). Therefore, the story of who the person is and the meaning given to his or her experience of sexual abuse is owned, operated, and told through the professional expert's meaning and knowledge about a generalized abuse experience.[11] A hierarchy of "truth" and knowledge is the result, and this can deny the storytelling rights of the person who endured the experience of sexual abuse.

A hierarchy of truth and knowledge is often isomorphic to the experience that the subject of abuse endured at having her storytelling rights denied and manipulated by the perpetrator of the abuse. Amanda Kamsler (1990), an early narrative therapy student of White, noted a number of storytelling practices associated specifically with child sexual abuse that deny the abused their own storytelling rights (A. Kamsler, personal communication, 1991, 1993) as follows:

---

[11] Our system of institutional values often privileges the expert's knowledge over the client's knowledge regarding the meaning of the abuse experience and the meaning of the person's response to this abuse experience.

(1) It is usually the case that the perpetrator of the abuse has overtly or covertly conveyed to the victim the message that she was to blame for being abused, (2) the perpetrator will often actively promote secrecy by enforcing it with the child or young woman so that she is divided from other family members, (3) and the various ways in which the perpetrator exerted control over the child . . . may promote the development of habitual responses of fear and panic in intimacy relationships when she becomes an adult. (pp. 17–18)

A person's story, the influences that shaped this story, and the right to tell this story from multiple perspectives are at the center of narrative therapy practice (Epston & White, 1992; White, 2004). As Michael White (personal communication, 1992, 2006) explained it, he spliced together Bateson's ideas of restraints together with Foucault's poststructuralist ideas on the constitutive notion of power/knowledge and ended up with the idea that the stories we hold and tell about our lives and relationships are solely developed in the context of certain prevailing ideologies (viewed as sociopolitical and cultural stories).[12] Theoretically, this was the backdrop to support his therapeutic method of externalizing internalized problem conversations (Madigan, 1992, 1996).

White's groundbreaking work of externalizing problems set out to deconstruct 150 years of psychological theory and practice landscape. Externalizing conversations simply questioned the contextual, cultural, and dialogic basis for why therapists were (universally) locating and privatizing problems inside the client's body—thereby creating a culture of the docile, disembodied, disempowered, unaffected, relational subject (Madigan, 1992). The utility and understanding of externalizing conversations relocates problems inside the relational and interactional context of culture and discourse and removes problems from the privacy of the decontextualized client body.

Karl Tomm described externalizing conversations as a "major achievement" and a "tour de force" (White & Epston, 1990). Tomm also warned

---

[12] For example, White brought to our attention that in relation to incest, dominant knowledges that influence women in the construction of their identities are imbedded within patriarchal ideology and helped along through popular forms of psychiatry that diagnose and classify. White viewed these ideologies as constructed within traditional linguistic and epistemological contexts in which incest has traditionally been located, written, and treated.

the field that to view White's externalizing practice as merely a therapeutic maneuver or technique would be both naive and limiting (K. Tomm, personal communication, 1990).

Michael White's practice of externalizing internalized problem discourse (Madigan, 1991a) put the politics of poststructural ideas (specifically those conceived of by Michel Foucault regarding the three modes of objectification of the subject and the inseparability of power and knowledge [Madigan, 1992], which I discuss later in the book) at the very heart of therapeutic practice for the first time in therapy's history. To the untrained structuralist/humanist eye, White's therapeutic performance could appear simplistic or gimmicky, yet when the therapist situates externalizing internalized problem discourse under the influence of poststructural ideas, the remarkable elegance of the practice comes rushing to life.

Michael White's (1988/1989) close-up reading of Michel Foucault allowed him to explore, theoretically, the therapeutic question, Is the talk about the problem gaining more influence over the person or is the person's talk gaining more influence over the problem?

White's consideration of this somewhat innocent puzzle led him to discover not only the oppressive effects that result from the ways in which problems are usually discussed but also the constitutive and subjugating effects of descriptive knowledge and language itself (M. White, personal communication, June 1990).White's therapeutic practice of externalizing a person's problem discourse set out to separate the person/client from the problem and/or the restraints that maintained the dominant discourse (problematic stories) about the problem. In Michael White's therapeutic world, the problem was located outside the person or relationship that had been objectified, identified, and specified (as having the problem), and the problem itself was objectified and given a relational name (White, 1989).

## DEMYSTIFYING PROBLEMS

Epston and White worked to relationally demystify problems by resisting the systemic temptation to totalize persons within a problem description. This expression of their poststructural commitments afforded them an ability to look past the restraints that made the person's story stagnant. Accordingly, they found new conversational pathways through the restraints (by exploring discursive double descriptions, unique outcomes, etc.). They developed this crucial therapeutic idea further by beginning to more fully understand Foucault's ideas on (a) what cultural and discursive restraints were, (b) how they operated on persons and how persons responded to them, (c) through which institutions they originated, and (d) who and what supported them.

From this emerging narrative therapy perspective, they realized that the professional stories we told about clients and problems were not as "factual" or "natural" as the field believed. They found that the prevailing ways of describing clients were culture-based constructs shaped by larger institutional knowledges like religion, media, psychiatry, education, law, science, and government. They also realized that the majority of our psychological practice ideas were not truths but taken-for-granted ideas produced through the institution's knowledge/power practices and consequently reproduced by the citizenry (e.g., of psychology).

For example, Epston and White began to question how a large majority of therapists were locating what was newly being called *attention-deficit/hyperactivity disorder (ADHD)* directly inside a young person's body (thereby leaving any contextual factors outside the diagnosis/story being told). They perceived that the hard and fast ideas being inscribed on the young person's body/identity were historical and had been negotiated throughout many different cultural arenas.[13]

---

[13] As far back as the conclusion of the Conference on Stimulant Use in the Treatment of ADHD in San Antonio, December 10–12, 1996, there were questions as to ADHD's sudden and successful rise. According to a statement by the deputy assistant administrator in the Office of Diversion Control at the Drug Enforcement Administration, "Today, we have concluded a national conference of experts from the fields of research, medicine, public health and law enforcement brought together by the U.S. Drug Enforcement Administration (DEA) to examine issues concerning the prescribing of stimulants to school-age children for the treatment of Attention Deficit Hyperactive Disorder (Attention Deficit Hyperactivity Disorder, ADHD, ADD/ADHD, attention deficit hyperactive disorder, attention deficit hyperactivity disorder). The principal drug used for this purpose is methylphenidate, commonly known as 'Ritalin.' The DEA has become alarmed by the tremendous increase in the prescribing of these drugs in recent years. Since 1990, prescriptions for methylphenidate have increased by 500 percent, while prescriptions for amphetamine for the same purpose have increased 400 percent." The report went on to state that "from seven to ten percent of the nation's boys are on these drugs at some point as well as a rising percentage of girls. When so many children are involved in the daily use of such a powerful psychoactive drugs, it is important for all of us to understand what is going on and why."

Historically, narrative therapy has argued that there are always multiple stories (multiple meanings) about what and who persons and problems might be.[14] So right from the start, White and Epston found that they had landed in some rather choppy and unchartered therapeutic waters. Their rather alienated experience of therapy was supported within the mandate of the dominant professional, psychological discipline of helping, and there wasn't a previous practice map to configure a new consideration of the poststructural, multistoried, dialogic self.

Finding themselves on the "outs" with psychological, psychiatric, and social work thinking (and the institutions that support these fields), they found a conspiratorial kinship with the emerging postmodern era and the many challenges being launched against the liberal and Enlightenment frameworks of understanding (Sampson, 1993). These postmodern ideological challenges were at the same time rocking the established schools of philosophy, literary criticism, and human sciences, including anthropology, sociology, and psychology. In dispute were the many assumed understandings of a unified description of the self, identity, and subjectivity.

The women's movement[15] also mobilized behind these challenges of dominant and fixed notions of the self (regarding who women were and who they were being defined as and by whom; Speedy, 2004; Swan, 1998). The social movements involving people of color (civil rights), people with different sexual orientations (gay rights), along with antipoverty/social housing activists, and so forth, had also risen up to confront various taken-for-granted ideas about personhood. And although each movement had its specific agendas and goals, all joined together to question the self-celebratory (Sampson, 1993) domination and monologic[16] formulation carried out by the dominant groups (White and privileged male). This dominant group had, up until this point in the history of the West, completely defined who

---

[14]Keeping this in mind, it's a bit tricky for any professional to make any attempt at trying to pin a person's identity down into a unified definition (for example a *Diagnostic and Statistical Manual of Mental Disorders* diagnosis) or to believe their expert opinion is the truth.

[15]The Just Therapy Team and Cheryl White were influential in bringing Epston and White toward accessing feminist ideas and critique.

[16]For an interesting review on the difference between monologic and dialogic conversations, see Madigan and Epston's 1995 paper titled "From 'Spychiatric Gaze' to Communities of Concern—From Monologue to Dialogues."

and what it was to be "normal," what constituted a self, what a person's or group's preferred roles were supposed to be, and the real quantifiable identity of the other. The "othered" group (othered by the dominant groups definition and clearly defined as other than a member of the dominant group) began to support this "otherness" of themselves through a dialogic alternative.

Narrative therapy found great solace in the challenges being brought forward. Subsequently, White and Epston's practice of therapy was, through the course of time, strongly influenced by feminism; gay rights/queer theory; and a postcolonial analysis of racism, class, and the notion of power and structural inequalities (M. White, personal communication, 2004). Up to this point in the history of therapy, an analysis of power relations had not yet surfaced (M. White, personal communication, 1990).

The issues of power relations, structural inequalities, and ownership of the storytelling rights of personhood are central to the work of narrative therapy.[17] These social-justice based positions/questions were given their initial push forward into narrative therapy practice understanding under the tutelage of the Just Therapy Team[18] of Wellington, New Zealand (Tamasese & Waldegrave, 1990). The Just Therapy Team not only spoke openly and directly to the promotion of these ideas[19] but also wrote about them (in the Dulwich Centre's narrative therapy journal; Waldegrave, 1990) and organized their "multicultural agency" practice through them.

The Just Therapy Team's discussions involved an outline of how othered marginalized groups desired a genuine alternative therapeutic dialogue. Marginalized groups (e.g., women, people of color, persons living in poverty, and persons struggling with mental health issues, disabilities) no longer wanted to be dictated to or told who they actually were as persons, as defined by the dominant class of Western psychological thinking (T. K.

---

[17] Epston and White's theoretical and therapy practices were heavily influenced by a group of American anthropologists that included Clifford Geertz, Barbara Myerhof, and Victor Turner; psychologists Jerome Bruner and Ken Gergen; and French philosophers Jacque Derrida and Michel Foucault.

[18] The Just Therapy Team members were the first therapists within the narrative camp to publicly discuss these therapeutic ideas in workshops

[19] In the first international narrative therapy conference sponsored by the Vancouver School for Narrative Therapy in 1993 in Vancouver, Canada, the Just Therapy Team gave the keynote address on gender, race, and power relations in therapy—outlining their Just Therapy approach to North America for the first time. See http://www.therapeuticconversations.com.

Tamasese and C. Waldegrave, personal communication, 1991, 1996, 2004, 2008). The Just Therapy Team's dialogic challenge reflected a mass dissatisfaction with psychologies monologic noncontextualized accounting of human experience.[20] These ideas moved White and Epston even further toward seeing the value of countering and resisting present-day psychological therapy practices.

Over a few short years (1982–1988), White and Epston managed to create a uniquely innovative therapy map to incorporate this newly found therapeutic interpretation of the multistoried and othered self (White, 2002). This process involved asking questions regarding how (and through what contexts) the person (and all those lending a discursive hand in the construction of the person and problem identity) came to tell, take up, and perform the problem story being told.

For example, the narrative therapy concept of *re-storying*[21] assists the person, or groups of persons, who has experienced trauma and abuse to avoid being restrained by another person's finalized account of who they have been, who they presently are, and who they might become (Denborough, 2008). Story lines told in a problem-saturated way may omit an analysis of power relations and any appreciative version of the person (and his or her context) that has been subjected to abuse. The content of this restrained and regressive narrative of persons who have been subjected to trauma and abuse is often supported by the perpetrator, media accounts, and judicial statements (Wade, 1996), as well as by discourse contained with therapeutic, medical, and legal texts (Jenkins, 1990, 2009; Wade, 1996).

As an alternative, White and Epston's narrative therapy offered a dialogic forum to bring forth untold stories of appreciation and respect regarding how the person responded to and survived the abusive context (Bird, 2000; Jenkins, 1990; Wade, 1997; White, 2002). Narrative therapy conversations were constructed to include an exploration of the person's

---

[20] For example, the Just Therapy Team's research is interested in the many cultural factors that may relationally influence such "phenomenon" as homelessness, violence, and poverty.

[21] The therapeutic notion of re-storying creates the possibility that change is always possible. Therefore, any totalized description of a person (i.e., as chronic) is perceived as a professional description that defines change as not possible. Chronic descriptions of life find a difficult fit within the practice of narrative therapy and the concept of re-storying (see Epston, 1986).

specific abilities that were used in order to survive the abusive context (e.g., becoming invisible, having relationships with anger and drugs, remaining silent, running way); appreciated the power-over tactics they suffered under threat of the larger, older, and stronger perpetrator (Jenkins, 2009); reviewed a context of imbalanced gender relations (Augusta-Scott, 2007); and discovered accomplishments people had made in their lives despite the torture they endured. These conversations (known to narrative therapy as *re-authoring conversations*) afforded a dialogic balance to the problem/person description/interpretation and a reconfigured abusive context (that assists people out of the constraints of the predominant problem-saturated stories of passivity, shame, and less-than worthiness, etc.; Bird, 2000; Epston, 1988; White 1991, 2002).

## TRAVELS WITH TOM

By way of reintroducing you to Tom, I remind you that after the psychiatric ward referred him to me, Tom, through a slurred medicated speech, relayed that he had ended up on the "crazy ward" because he'd been feeling "depressed" since his retirement at age 65 (one and a half years earlier). He also said that he had twice tried to "off" (kill) himself "without success" (once before his admittance into the hospital and once during his stay in the hospital).

At the beginning of the first interview, I asked Tom if the word *depressed* was a term of his own or if it belonged to someone else. He responded that it was a "hospital word" and what he was "really feeling" was "bored and unaccomplished." In the first session, I raised a few suspicions with Tom by asking him a small number of the following counter-viewing questions (Tom's answers are in parentheses):

Tom, do you think this bored and unaccomplished sense of yourself is a final description of yourself? (Maybe not.)

Tom, why do you think this bored and unaccomplished sense of yourself may not be a final description of yourself? (It might be the shock treatment, because it makes me slow and I can't remember much. I retired and didn't know what to do and I feel like a rock on the end of a piece of rope.)

What does feeling like a rock on the end of a rope feel like? (Lousy, like I have nowhere to turn—just hanging here.)

Is there someplace you would rather be? (As the bumper sticker on my car says—I'd rather be gardening.)

And what would you grow? (I'm not sure the hospital would let me grow anything.)

Tom, if you get back to growing up things in your life, what would you grow? (I'd like to grow heirloom tomatoes again and see all their weird colors and shapes and maybe watch my grandkids grow.)

If you were able to take this step to grow a bit of yourself back, what do you believe you might be stepping toward? (I'd get myself out of the madhouse!)

Is there one particular aspect of yourself that most wants and supports you to move out of the madhouse? (The part of me that wants to be free.)

Can you remember a time in your recent or distant past when you felt that you were free? (Yes, many times like when I was gardening and when I was playing hockey with my old friends on Tuesday nights or even just shoveling the snow off the driveway.)

The session continued as follows:

Tom, is the hospital's description of you as a chronically depressed person an accurate description of you? (No, I think they helped me get worse.)

In what ways do you feel that the hospital has made you feel worse about yourself? (Well, being with them a year or so I haven't gotten any better, and I think that they are giving up—this is why they sent me to you [laughs]—you're the last stop and they weren't much help anyway. Most of them are nice, but you know.)

Tom, do you think the hospital staff is a little confused because they think maybe by coming to talk with me they have developed some hope for you? (Well, they told me you helped someone else like me, so yes.)

Why do you think they think and hope that I can help you and they can't? (Because I don't think they know what they are doing, and I get mad at them for shocking me as much as they did.)

Jane (Tom's partner of 40 years), are you mad at them for shocking Tom as well? (Yes, I am mad, and I am glad we are here because my sister's niece told her that you were different.)

Tom, do you think Jane thinks there is hope that you can overcome this unaccomplished boredom? (Yes.)

Can I ask you if Jane has said or done anything recently to help you believe that she believes this? (Jane always says I'll get better, and she tells other people I will—but I don't know.)

Who are these other people in your life that you think might be pinning their hopes on you beating this boredom? (Ah, there are quite a few of them, I think.)

Can you name a few of these hopeful people? (Well, my kids, and the neighbors and I don't know, Jane, and the occupational therapist.)

Do you have any ideas about what all of these people witness and remember in you that you have lately somehow forgotten about in yourself? (The shocks have made me forgetful, but maybe they could tell you a thing or two.)

Tom, do you feel that there might be aspects of who you are—as a man and a husband, father, employer, friend, worker, and gardener—that you once enjoyed but now these other yous have somehow fallen into silence? (Maybe, yes they are there—but like hidden.)[22]

It was through sets of questions that certain hospital certainties as well as the problem's saturation were undermined as a means to open space for other possibilities and discontinuities constituting the storied inscription of Tom. The therapeutic re-authoring conversations between Tom, Jane, and myself tracked the threads of the institution's discursive practices and destabilized the hard chronic conclusions placed on Tom's body. In taking away expert knowledge from the site of the hospital, we enlarged the degree to which alternative other insider knowledges (e.g., those of Tom and Jane, their family members) might be taken up, privileged, retold, and performed.

Throughout our sessions, Tom and Jane began to inscribe themselves back toward local, historical, cultural, and social knowledges lost to them within the problem and professional discourse and through the vast array

---

[22] The reader will note that under the process of counterviewing questions, nothing was externalized. In fact, there are sometimes entire therapy sessions in which (traditional) relational externalizing conversations are not entered into.

of cultural discourse surrounding the person who retires. With their guidance, I witnessed how subversive responses were possible under even the most oppressive conditions. Our conversations afforded forms of resistance and transformation that were historical processes. We analyzed and counterviewed various discourses and began to situate the discursive threads of retirement, shock treatment, men's identities, psychiatry, fatherhood, and relationships.

Foucault emphasized that power relations are never seamless but always spawning new forms of culture and subjectivity and new opportunities for transformation. Where there is power, he came to see, there is also resistance (Dreyfus & Rabinow, 1983). Dominant forms of knowledge and the institutions that support them are continually being penetrated and reconstructed by values, styles, and knowledges that have been developing and gathering strength at the margins.

The more our (Tom, Jan, myself, and others) readings of the dominant/normative textual tellings were investigated, the more we seemed to position against the grain of the popular, the taken-for-granted, and the chronic. As we moved away from the disciplinary practices of living as a retired depressed/hospitalized person, the more Tom began to gain back aspects of himself once forgotten through the "shock" of retirement, the subsequent boredom (after having had a work identity since he was 13 years old), and the loss of his remembered alternative self being replaced with strong feelings of an unaccomplished life.

Tom's rediscovery[23] was helped along, in part, through counterviewing narrative interviews and a very intense 30-person therapeutic letter writing campaign (see a description in Chapter 4). It was through sets of discursive counterviewing questions that certain hospital certainties were undermined as a way to open space for other possibilities and discontinuities constituting the storied inscription of Tom.

The therapeutic conversations between Tom, Jane, and me tracked the threads of the institutions discursive practices and destabilized the

---

[23]*Rediscovery* is a word I learned from the Vancouver Anti-Anorexia/Bulimia League. It was through words like this that they attempted to reinvent their own language; in this case, they wanted to take back the word *recovery* and substitute it with what they called a less encumbered or cleaner word, which was *rediscovery*.

hard chronic conclusions placed on Tom's body. As mentioned previously, by taking away expert knowledge from the site of the hospital, we enlarged the degree to which alternative other knowledges might be taken up and performed.

One day (about 6 months after he released himself from the psychiatric hospital), Tom brought me a gift he had designed for the Vancouver School for Narrative Therapy. The charcoal painting read "Negative Imagination Only Remembers Negative Events." Tom continues to garden his heirloom tomatoes and has now included a particularly spicy salsa garden in his earthy repertoire.

# Theory

*There is no power relation without the correlative constitution of a field of knowledge, nor any knowledge that does not presuppose and constitute at the same time power relations.*
—Michel Foucault (*Discipline and Punish: The Birth of the Prison*)

## A MULTISTORIED VERSION OF LIFE

By taking up a poststructural theoretical view, Epston and White proposed that the complexity of life, and how lives are lived, is mediated through the expression of the stories we tell. Stories are shaped by the surrounding dominant cultural context; some stories emerge as the long-standing reputations we live through, and other (often more preferred) stories of who we are (and might possibly become) can sometimes be restrained and pushed back to

---

Portions of this chapter have been excerpted or adapted from handouts created by Stephen Madigan for use in his workshops at the Therapeutic Conversations conferences.

the margins of our remembered experience (Madigan, 1992, 2008). But whatever the stories are that we tell (and don't tell), they are performed, live through us, and have abilities to both restrain and liberate our lives (Epston, 2009; Parker, 2008; Turner, 1986; White, 1995a, 2002).

White and Epston organized their therapy practice around the idea of a multistoried version of life (of what a story/problem-story can mean). This therapeutic concept afforded them the flexibility to view persons and problems not as fixed, fossilized, or under any one unitary description, theory, or label (White & Epston, 1990; White, 2002). Multistoried considerations regarding who a person might be in relation to the problem allowed them to reconsider and resist an isolated or categorized story of a person.[1]

Epston and White's narrative therapy afforded the person and/or problem definition a flexibility for multiple interpretations of what he or she might be—allowing both client and therapist the possibility to re-vise, re-collect, and re-member (McCarthy, personal communication, 1998; Meyerhoff, 1986; White, 1979) a story from various and competing perspectives (Madigan, 1996; Madigan & Epston, 1995; White, 2005). It is among these relational re-authoring conversations that change was believed to take place in narrative therapy (Dickerson & Zimmerman, 1996).

Epston and White also believed that a multistoried version of life might include a newly revised re-telling about a person's and/or group's past, present, and future (Denborough, 2008). For example, in 1974, millions of Americans were deemed healthy (literally) overnight when the diagnostic category *homosexuality* was erased from the American Psychiatric Association's (APA) *Diagnostic and Statistical Manual of Mental Disorders (DSM)*. At that time, the American Psychiatric Association made headlines by announcing that it had decided homosexuality was no longer a mental illness. The decision was brought forward as gay activists demonstrated in front of the American Psychiatric Association convention. The 1974 vote

---

[1] Common solitary story lines of people who come to therapy include over-involved mother, under-involved man, despondent immigrant worker, anorexic girl, depressed sole parent, oppositional youth—and any universally agreed-on description acting to harden the categories of what can be storied and/or given relevance.

showed 5,854 association members supporting and 3,810 opposing the disorder's removal from the manual.

From a narrative therapy perspective, the practice of voting on whether homosexuality constitutes mental illness is not only therapeutically absurd but, needless to say, also highly unscientific and politically motivated (J. Tilsen, personal communication, 2006). Narrative therapists regard the vote on the status of gay identity as a clear example of how illogical it is for professionals in positions of power to be allowed to make arbitrary decisions regarding the mental health identity of others (Caplan, 1995; Nylund, Tilsen, & Grieves, 2007). Nevertheless, with the stroke of a powerfully political pen, these identified homosexual persons, once viewed as sick and/or morally evil by professional members of psychiatry, religion, the law, and so on, were moved (at least by the American Psychiatric Association) from one side of the healthy/unhealthy binary to the other (however, they remained unholy and unlawful in the eyes of many religious institutions and legal jurisdictions).

The politics of such a move are quite telling about how psychological decisions regarding healthy/unhealthy identities are willfully created in the fields of mental health. The politics of psychiatry's power-over position also demonstrates the capricious and half-baked intellectual scenery of psychological decision making.

As witnesses to this process of documentation within psychological history, we might now turn our sights toward how other categories of pathology are invented. For example, we might question what institutional processes are involved in turning so-called healthy persons into supposed unhealthy and not "normal" members of society (Nylund & Corsiglia, 1993, 1994, 1996). The answer to this question regarding the legitimacy of a person's identity may depend on who is telling this story, from what set of ethical beliefs they are telling the story from, and with what authority they are telling it. The conclusion is often our realization that not all stories told are equal. However, the power to advise or label someone (and through this process decide who is normal and who is not normal) is often a source of unquestioned authority and privilege by both professionals and those who seek our help.

From the outset, narrative therapy has explored the issue of storytelling rights with people and the influence this may have in constructing a life support system for problems (M. White, personal communication, 1990). Take, for example, the story that a sole parent and immigrant mother recently told me about how, during a 15-minute physical checkup with her new general practitioner, she was informed that she was a "depressed" person. Despite the medical doctor's psychological diagnosis proving to be shocking news for the woman, she did adhere to the culturally sanctioned medical/psychological expertise by purchasing the selective serotonin reuptake inhibitor medication prescribed. It was through the mediated politics of this (somewhat common) power-related medical interchange that she then began to question her own version of herself (as healthy and well functioning). When I asked her how she currently viewed herself, she responded that she had begun the process of performing herself as a depressed person.

By reproducing the professional's opinion of her as a depressed person (as a more relevant and complete story of who she was), the woman began to question her reputation as a community leader within her cultural group, as a strong survivor within her family, as a loving parent to her children, and as a skilled worker to her employer. Unfortunately, these community-supported stories of herself were not accounted for by the doctor during their 15-minute problem-focused depression interview.

Without an exploration by the family doctor into the *intersectionality*[2] of the woman's personhood—living outside the boundaries and confinements of the disembodied category of depression—the relationship between depression and the person was left vastly underexplored. Naming the woman's experience *depression* and having the professional expert's story individually inscribed onto her body did absolutely nothing to account for a relational and contextual exploration of other relevant issues such as gender, race, sexuality, class, and so forth. To a narrative

---

[2] Intersectionality is a sociological theory seeking to examine how various socially and culturally constructed categories of discrimination interact on multiple and often simultaneous levels, contributing to systematic social inequality. Intersectionality holds that the classical models of oppression within society, such as those based on race/ethnicity, gender, religion, nationality, sexual orientation, class, or disability, do not act independently of one another; instead, these forms of oppression interrelate, creating a system of oppression that reflects the "intersection" of multiple forms of discrimination.

therapist, a noncontextualized therapeutic interview of this kind would be viewed as unethical.

## RE-AUTHORING CONVERSATIONS

Psychologist Jerome Bruner[3] (1990) suggested that within our selection of stories expressed, there are always feelings and lived experience left out of the dominant story told. Narrative therapy is organized through the text analogy, with the central idea that it is the stories people tell and hold about their lives that determine the meaning they give to their lives. Therefore, it is what we select out as meaningful from the stories we tell that is given expression. For example, a grade of 80% on a driving test could be expressed through a story of appreciating what was remembered in order to achieve an 80% passing grade or, alternatively, what it was that accounted for all that was forgotten that did not afford a perfect grade—two descriptions and two very different experiences in the telling of these descriptions.

Epston and White relied heavily on the text analogy (J. Bruner, 1990) as a way to explore re-authoring conversations[4] with the people who came to see them in therapy. Re-authoring conversations were a crucial part of both the philosophical underpinnings of narrative therapy theory as well as the practice work itself. White and Epston found that persons tended to seek out therapy when the narratives they were telling (or were somehow involved in) did not quite represent their lived experience and when there were vital aspects of their experience that contradicted dominant narratives about them (D. Epston, personal communication, 1991). They found that by externalizing problems, the process assisted persons in separating from saturated tellings of these problem stories. Persons then began to identify previously neglected aspects of their lived experience (that contradicted the dominant story told).

---

[3] J. Bruner suggested that there are two primary modes of thought: the narrative mode and the paradigmatic mode. In narrative thinking, the mind engages in sequential, action-oriented, detail-driven thought. In paradigmatic thinking, the mind transcends particularities to achieve systematic, categorical cognition. In the former case, thinking takes the form of stories and "gripping drama."

[4] The text analogy proposes that meaning is derived from storying our experience. And it is the stories that persons tell that determine meaning about their lives.

Epston and White also found that re-authoring conversations invited people to do what they routinely do, that is, to link events of their lives in sequences through time—according to a theme or a specific plot (J. Bruner, 1990). It was in this activity of telling/performing their story that people were assisted by the therapist to identify the more neglected events of their lives, named in narrative therapy as *unique outcomes*[5] (Goffman, 1961). People were then encouraged to capture these unique outcomes into alternative story lines named *unique accounts*. For example, when Tom (see Chapter 2, this volume) first entered into therapy with me, he initially relayed a version of himself as a "failed" person. It was only after a bit of narrative inquiry that he began a fascinating re-telling of himself that included stories about his life lived as a proud father, fair-minded employer, talented gardener, etc.— stories once restrained through a totalized telling of himself as a resident-psychiatric-ward-chronic-problem person.

White and Epston (1990) felt that unique outcomes provided a starting point for re-authoring conversations that lived outside the restraints of the problem-saturated story being told. Unique outcomes made available a point of entry into the alternative story lines of people's lives that, at the outset of these therapeutic conversations, became visible only as withered traces that were full of gaps and not clearly named. As these conversations proceeded, therapists built a scaffold around the emerging subordinate story (M. White, personal communication, 1991).

As unique outcomes were identified, the narrative therapy conversation plotted them into an alternative story line about the person's lived experience. Unique outcomes were explained by way of unique accounts as the narrative therapist worked to generate questions to produce, locate, and resurrect alternative (and preferred) stories that filled in—and made more sense of—the client's stories of unique outcomes (White, 1988/1989).

Questions were introduced by Epston and White to investigate what these new developments in the story might mean about the person and his or her relationships (stories that lived outside the dominant-problem story

---

[5]Unique outcomes are also referred to as *exceptions*. Unique accounts of these unique outcomes are also referred to as, for example, alternative stories or subordinate storylines.

being told by the person, family members, or professional). It was then important to the therapeutic conversation for these subordinate stories to be given a thicker description (Geertz, 1983) and plotted into an alternative story about the person's life.

More questions might be crafted to inspire what White and Epston (1990) called *unique redescription questions*[6] designed to investigate what the new developments might reflect about the person and his or her relationships. Questions also involved the investigation of plot lines to discover unique outcomes, unique accounts, unique possibilities, and unique circulations of the story, as well as experience of experiences, preferences, and historical locations to support the evolving story (I explore these questions further in Chapter 4).

The numerous ways that Epston and White designed narrative therapy's re-authoring conversations acted to re-invigorate people's efforts to understand (a) what it was that was happening in their lives, (b) what it was that had happened, (c) how it had happened, and (d) what it all could possibly mean. In this way, therapeutic conversations encouraged a dramatic reengagement with life and with history and provided options for people to more fully inhabit their lives and their relationships.

Epston and White established that there were some parallels between the skills of re-authoring conversations and the skills required to produce texts of literary merit.[7] Among other things, texts of literary merit encourage (in the reader) a dramatic reengagement with many of their own experiences of life. It is within this dramatic reengagement that the gaps in the story line are filled, and the person lives the story by taking it over as his or her own.

Operating alongside the skills that construct texts of literary merit, White and Epston made it possible for people to address and to fill in the gaps of these alternative landscapes of their experience (Epston, 1998). Their narrative therapy questions were not oriented to the already known in ways that precipitated the sort of thoughtlessness that is the outcome of

---

[6] See Chapter 4 on unique redescription questions.

[7] White and Epston's book *Narrative Means to Therapeutic Ends* was originally published in 1990 as *Literary Means to Therapeutic Ends*.

boredom and an acute familiarity with the subject,[8] and nor were these narrative questions oriented to precipitate the sort of thoughtlessness that is the outcome of fatigue and of failure to identify the unfamiliar.[9]

As re-authoring conversations evolved, they provided conditions under which it became possible for people to step into the near future of the landscapes of action of their lives (Epston & Roth, 1995). Questions were introduced that encouraged people to (a) generate new proposals for action, (b) account for the circumstances likely to be favorable to these proposals for action, and (c) predict the outcome of these proposals.

Epston and White found that people were likely to respond to questions by generating identity conclusions that were informed by the well-known structuralist categories of identity—these being categories of needs, motives, attributes, traits, strengths, deficits, resources, properties, characteristics, drives, and so on. These structuralist identity conclusions invariably provided a poor basis for knowledge of how to proceed in life. As these conversations further evolved, there were opportunities for people to generate identity conclusions that were informed by nonstructuralist categories of identity—intentions and purposes, values and beliefs, hopes, dreams and visions, commitments to ways of living, and so on (M. White, personal communication, 1992, Adelaide, South Australia).

It was in the context of the development of these nonstructuralist identity conclusions that people found the opportunity to progressively distance themselves from their problemed lives, and it was from this distance that they became knowledgeful about matters of how to proceed (D. Epston, personal communication, 2009). It was also from this distance that people found the opportunity to have significant dramatic engagements with their own lives and to take further steps in the occupancy and habitation of their life.[10]

---

[8] A narrative therapist is interested in having completely new and novel conversations in therapy with the person. This involves a new re-telling of the story of the person/problem and not a parroting of what has been told many times before by the person or by experts commenting on the person/problem relationship.

[9] As in the development of any skills, competence in the expression of these scaffolding questions is acquired through practice, more practice, and then more practice.

[10] Some material in this section has been reprinted from *Workshop Notes*, by M. White, September 21, 2005, and retrieved from http://www.dulwichcentre.com.au/michael-white-workshop-notes.pdf. Copyright 2005 by the Dulwich Centre. Reprinted with permission.

## TWO MODES OF DESCRIPTION

American psychologist Jerome Bruner[11] (1986, 1990) wrote that there are two modes of contrasting thought within the social sciences: thought informed by positivist science and thought informed by a narrative mode of thinking. He suggested that there are two modes of cognitive functioning, two modes of thought, and that each provides unique ways of ordering experience and constructing reality. Bruner believed that a good story and a well-formed argument were different natural kinds and that each could be used as a means for convincing another. Yet what they convince of is fundamentally different: Arguments convince one of their truth, stories of their lifelikeness. The one verifies by eventual appeal to procedures for establishing formal and empirical truth, and the other establishes not truth but verisimilitude (J. Bruner, 1986, p. 11).

Philosopher Paul Ricoeur (1984) suggested that it is the human condition to tell stories that narrative is built on. Furthering this line of thought, J. Bruner (1986) claimed that there is a certain "heartlessness" involved with empirical scientific logic. He wrote that because one is trained to move always in the direction of where one's premises, conclusions, and observations take them, one can thereby overlook certain intimate particularities of interaction. J. Bruner (1990) argued instead for an "imaginative application of the narrative mode," which deals with the gripping drama of good stories, and the "human or human-like intention and action and the vicissitudes and consequences that mark their course" (p. 13).

It is logico-scientific thought that is considered legitimate within the scientific community, as well as many segments of the social science community. This paradigm is based on an acquisition of "empirical discovery guided by reasoned hypothesis, and is directed towards finding universal truths as opposed to truth conditions" (J. Bruner, 1990, p. 14). This particular belief

---

[11] Although Bruner helped create the foundational work for cognitive–behavioral therapy, he later moved more toward a narrative mode of thinking. Bruner argued that the cognitive revolution, with its current fixation on mind as "information processor," has led psychology away from the deeper objective of understanding mind as a creator of meanings. He suggested that only by breaking out of the limitations imposed by a computational model of mind can we grasp the special interaction through which mind both constitutes and is constituted by culture. Bruner's ideas had a tremendous influence on David Epston and Michael White's development of narrative therapy.

is explained and popularized by a Western version of what and who constitutes the psychological subject (Sampson, 1989).

Within psychological science, persons are viewed as self-contained individuals who can be empirically studied, whereby laws concerning the "essence" of the individual can be invented, voted on, and universalized. Technologies and categories can then be put in place to keep models of theory and mental hygiene consistent through time (K. Tomm, personal communication, 1996; Caplan, 1991).

## TEXTUAL IDENTITY OF PERSONS

Through the text analogy, often referred to in terms of the narrative metaphor (E. M. Bruner, 1986; J. Bruner, 1991; White & Epston, 1990), social "scientists" came to the realization that they cannot have a direct knowledge of the world. Instead, they proposed a less fixed and rigid idea that persons know life through their storying of lived experience (J. Bruner, 1986, 1990; Geertz, 1973, 1976; Myerhoff, 1982; Turner, 1974, 1986). This story of lives through time is said to be performed (Turner, 1981) within a set of language rules or "games" (Wittgenstein, 1960, 1953). It is a person's storied discourse—a discourse shaped and spoken through a sociopolitical cultural context—that eventually determines the meaning given to an experience[12] (Butler, 1997; Said, 2003; Spivak, 1996).

The idea of the textual identity of the person[13] prompts a therapeutic shift from a vocabulary describing an object called the *self* to a vocabulary of self that describes the self as a product of changing social intercourse. This textual identity of the person rejects the following:

---

[12] Edward Bruner (1986) wrote about the recursive/reflexive relationship between discourse and performance; he noted that "the participants must have confidence in their own authenticity, which is one reason cultures are performed. It is not enough to assert claims; they must be enacted. Stories become transformative only in their performance" (p. 25).

[13] Kenneth Gergen (1991) questioned why we continue to perceive the point of origin behind a text to be located in the mind. He wrote: "If understanding a text is a matter of participating in on-going conventions of culture, then why is writing (or speaking) not a similar process—a matter of joining in the language games? To write or speak is not, then, to express an interior world, but to borrow from the available things people write and say and to reproduce from yet another audience" (K. Gergen, 1991, p. 105).

- notions of the self as an inner wealth of deep resources in combat with primitive impulses;
- ideas of a self alienated from a universe, an environment that it seeks to rejoin through rational comprehension of mysteries (scientific discovery) and through intense emotional attachments (romantic love);
- sense of self as a consistent, knowable, enduring identity (humanism) that is nurtured or limited and can be known, measured, and directed; and
- therapies of the self that focus on discovering historical (e.g., psychoanalysis) or environmental (e.g., behaviorism, systems) truths about the self and that relegate to themselves the power to set the self in new directions.

White and Epston's therapeutic reasoning shifted the focus of interpretation from the text and toward the interpretive strategies of the interpreter (Madigan, 1991a). The shift offered an alternative therapeutic position: that all statements postulating meaning are interpretive. They wrote the following: "Social scientists became interested in the text analogy following observations that, although a piece of behaviour occurs in time it is attended to, the meaning that is ascribed to the behaviour survives across time" (White & Epston, 1990, p. 9).

In their attempts to understand this idea, Epston and White began to invoke the text analogy, enabling the interaction of persons to be considered as the interaction of readers around particular texts. The analogy also made it possible to conceive of the evolution of lives and relationships in terms of the reading and writing of texts, insofar as every new reading of a text is a new interpretation of it, and thus a different writing of it.

The textual identity of persons supports the idea that all claims of meaning are interpretations embedded in specific cultural discourse and that all therapeutic constructions are culture specific (Waldegrave, 1990; C. Waldegrave, personal communication, 1991). Literary critic Stanley Fish (1980) proposed that in "literary interpretation the interpreting entity (or agent), endowed with purposes and concerns is, by virtue of its very operating, determining what *counts* as the facts observed" (p. 8). Therefore, it is the interpretive act that deconstructs any and all claims to certainty and truth about people and problems. For example, research shows that *DSM* reliability is poor and that two therapists are not likely to assign the same label (even for broad, not highly specific categories) to the same person (Breggin, 1994a; Caplan, 1995). Therefore, *DSM* research reliability proves suspect as the client being observed by the therapist is placed under each professional's interpretation.

White and Epston (1990) wrote that the "analogies we employ determine our examination of the world: the questions we ask about events, and the realities we construct . . . they determine the very distinctions that we pull out from the world" (p. 5). Their position supports Derrida's (1991) notion of preexisting frames and Madigan's (1991a) interpretive strategies of the interpreter. This then belies the question of what/which analogies, presuppositions, restraints, cultural knowledges, and other historically situated beliefs are involved in the professional positions a psychologist takes up with his or her client, the institutional ideas they are influenced by, and the general result that this has on the person's life and understanding of relationships and problems in therapy.

## MICHEL FOUCAULT

Any attempt at learning the primary theoretical understandings of narrative therapy practice can benefit from a brief review on a few of Michel Foucault's ideas.[14] Epston and White appropriated, reshaped, and mapped out many of Foucault's ideas onto the foundational practices of narrative therapy understanding (Madigan, 1992; White, 2005; White & Epston, 1990; Winslade, Crocket, Epston, & Monk, 1996).

Foucault wrote as both historian and philosopher,[15] and his polemic was raised against the practice of systematizing and universalizing certain political and scientific theories that act to turn people (subjects) into things (objects). He viewed a discourse that argued for the supremacy of one idea

---

[14] The first reference I have come across of a narrative therapist highlighting the work of Michel Foucault was a keynote address David Epston gave for the Australian Family Therapy Conference on September 24, 1983, in Brisbane, Australia.

[15] Many social science disciplines study Foucault's writings and consider him a leading intellectual voice of poststructuralism.

as a discourse of social control. Foucault's extensive collection of writings deconstructed many culturally constructed discourses and representations of what we as a society view as normal and abnormal among our community of individuals/citizens (Foucault, 1989, 1994b; Harstock, 1990; Madigan & Law, 1998; Parker, 2008).

Foucault was interested in how certain institutions introduced practices and structures to institute specific beliefs into scientific, psychological, religious, and moral law (Foucault, 1997). He studied institutions like psychiatric hospitals, prisons, and clinics and dismantled the "moral hygiene" they constructed to support prevailing institutional ideas regarding sex, sexuality, crime, and categories of mental illness. Foucault located historical strands of discourse and representations of discourse, which dealt not only with the subject but also with those practices involving the relationship of knowledge and power. In other words, his objective was to create a history pertinent to the different modes through which, in Western culture, human beings are objectified as subjects (Foucault, 1984a).

## DIVIDING PRACTICES

Foucault called the first mode of objectification of the subject a *dividing practice* (Foucault, 1965, 1977). Dividing practices are social and usually spatial: *social* in that people of a particular social grouping who exhibit difference could be subjected to certain means of objectification and *spatial* by being physically separated from the social group for exhibiting difference once identified. The actions of dividing practices are tolerated and justified through the mediation of science (or pseudoscience) and the power the social group gives to scientific claims. In this process of social objectification and categorization, human beings are given both a social and a personal identity. The leper colony is a cogent historical example of a dividing practice.

Foucault's research surveyed many historical examples of situations in which people specified by the state as abnormal had been spatially and socially divided. An example is the confinement of the poor, the insane, and the vagabonds in the great "catch-all" General Hospital in Paris in 1656.

Foucault argued that the classifications of disease from this time—and the associated practices of clinical medicine—influenced early 19th-century France and the rise of modern psychiatry as it was entered into the hospitals, prisons, and clinics throughout the 19th and 20th centuries. In addition, the medicalization, stigmatization, and normalization of sexual "deviance" in modern Europe were born out of these practices and have helped shape modern forms of living, law, and policymaking (Foucault, 1965, 1973, 1979). Current examples of dividing practices might include the objectification, isolation, and ghettoization (Hardy, 2004) of certain marginal groups such as ethnic minorities, persons with disabilities, and persons with AIDS.

## SCIENTIFIC CLASSIFICATION

Foucault (1983) referred to the second mode for turning human beings into objectified subjects as *scientific classification.* Foucault saw scientific classification as the practice of making the body a thing through, for example, the use of psychiatric diagnostic testing. *DSM* technology (among others) is utilized as a means for classification, and this action emerges from discourses that are produced and given the status of "science" (Foucault, 1983).

Foucault showed how, at different stages of history, certain scientific universals regarding human social life were held privileged. Through this privileged status, certain scientific classifications acted to specify social norms (Foucault, 1984b). Hence, socially produced specifications and categorizations of normal and abnormal personhood evolved and perpetuated universal classification in what Foucault called *totalization techniques* (culturally produced notions about the specification of personhood; Foucault, 1983). The cultural practice of specifying what constitutes the "normal employee" or, as Foucault (1983) wrote, the "subject who labors" is an example of a socially produced specification. Another example is the ongoing debate that surrounds the privileging of heteronormativity as the only relationship sanctioned by the state to legally marry (Simons, 1995; Tilsen & Nylund, 2009).

Another commonly used practice of classification is the documentation of lives, which became possible through the invention of files (e.g., medical, insurance, corporate, school). The file enabled individuals to be "captured" and fixed in time through writing and could be used to facilitate the gathering of statistics and the fixing of norms. The file could also be used as an instrument to promote the construction of unitary and global knowledges about people. This turning of real lives into writing was viewed by Foucault as a mechanism of social control.

## SUBJECTIFICATION

Foucault's (1983) third mode of objectification analyzes the ways in which human beings turn themselves into subjects. He called this third mode *subjectification.* This objectification of the subject is a process that differs significantly from the other two modes of objectification, in which the individual takes up a more passive, constrained position.

Foucault suggested that subjectification involves those processes of self-formation or identity in which the person is active. He was primarily concerned with isolating those techniques through which people initiate their own active self-formation. Subjectification, under the influence of internalized cultural discourse (see Madigan 2003, 2004, 2007), was viewed by Foucault as an action of self-control and guided by set social standards (Foucault, 1983). He suggested that people monitor and conduct themselves according to their interpretation of set cultural norms and that they also seek out external authority figures such as a religious leader or psychoanalyst for further guidance (Foucault, 1983, 1994b). Yet, however helpful these culturally produced bits of heavenly advice and transference interpretations might be, he made it clear that they are solely shaped by the prevailing cultural discourse.

Foucault contended that our self-formation is *performative.* This performative self-formation has a long and complicated history, as it takes place through a variety of operations on people's own bodies, thoughts, and conduct (Foucault, 1980; Turner, 1969, 1986). These operations characteristically entail a process of self-understanding through self-surveillance

(Madigan, 2007) and an active relational participation with internalized cultural dialogue mediated through prevailing external cultural norms (Foucault, 1980, 1983; Madigan, 2004, 2007, 2009). Foucault's position suggests that it is virtually impossible to be situated outside of culture in any action in which we partake.

His description of architect Jeremy Bentham's 17th-century Panopticon[16] is an example of the attempt by the state to control the subject through subject control (Foucault, 1979; O'Farrell, 2005). Here the Panopticon's structure and function serve to promote an externalized cultural (normative) gaze, which is internalized by the subject and moves the subject toward practices of the body deemed desirable by the culture of power (Prado, 1995).

The performance of self-surveillance (the self monitoring the self in relation to set cultural norms; see Madigan, 2004) can be explained as the performance of looking, monitoring, and judging the self (see Foucault 1965, 1979).[17] The monitoring of the self, eavesdropping on itself, is bound together in a dialogic relationship with an active audience discursively positioned elsewhere. Our experience of the imagined or recreated thoughts of the other looking, monitoring, and judging us (the other also includes ourselves looking at ourselves) is constitutive and reproducing of cultural normativity (Foucault 1973, 1989; Madigan, 1996, 1997; White, 1995a).

On the basis of Foucauldian notions of subjectification, Michael White (1997) elucidated an unholy trinity relating to popular humanist accounts of identity as follows: (a) a will to truth that supports ideas regarding our being, essence, or human nature; (b) the emancipation narrative that seeks to liberate the self from repression; and (c) a repressive hypothesis outlining how repression hides our essential nature and inhibits self-actualization.

---

[16] The Panopticon was a type of prison building designed by English philosopher and social theorist Jeremy Bentham in 1785. The concept of the design was to allow an observer to observe (-opticon) all (pan-) prisoners without the prisoners being able to tell whether they were being watched, thereby conveying what one architect has called the sentiment of an invisible omniscience. Bentham described the Panopticon as a new mode of obtaining power of mind over mind, in a quantity hitherto without example.

[17] For narrative therapy practice interpretations on the self-surveillance of the subject, see Madigan, 1992, 2004, 2008.

# THE INSEPARABILITY OF POWER
# AND KNOWLEDGE

Taken together, the three modes of objectification of the subject—(a) those that categorize, distribute, and manipulate; (b) those through which we have come to understand ourselves scientifically; and (c) those that we use to form ourselves into meaning-giving selves—designate the landscape of Foucault's inquiries and shape the foundation of narrative therapy inquiry.

Clustered tightly around the identity of the subject are the twin terms of *knowledge* and *power*.[18] The point to which Foucault consistently returned is the idea that there are no truths, only interpretations of truth. He specified that knowledges that make global truth claims are supported through knowledges of modern scientific disciplines. Foucault (1980) wrote that as

> "both participants and subjects of this power through knowledge, we are judged, condemned, classified, determined in our undertaking, destined to a certain mode of living or dying, as a function of the true discourses which are the bearers of the specific effects of power" (p. 94).

Foucault espoused the relational and constitutive dimension of power/knowledge (Foucault, 1980; McHoul & Grace, 1993). This suggests that all discursive practices (all the ways a culture creates social and psychological realities) are interpretations embedded in specific cultural discourse, in which the subject is considered created by, and creating of, the cultural discourse. Foucault's (1984a) conception of the inseparability of power/knowledge is reflected in his confrontation of those who argue for the ascendancy of a particular brand of knowledge over others. For example, the discourse of pharmaceutical medicine in relation to mental health is supported by a powerful industrial lobby and, over time, has begun to overshadow the practice and worth of talk therapy.

Foucault suggested that alternative knowledges that raise questions about prevailing ideas and practices are often silenced through their disqualification. Foucault called these disqualified knowledges *local knowledges.*

---

[18] Put simply, Foucault suggested that people do not "have" power implicitly; rather, power is a technique or an action that individuals can engage in.

Local knowledges are specific discursive practices that often contrast those cultural knowledges that survive and rise above. The latter he called *global knowledges* (discussing the complexity and curiosity between the relational interchange of local and global knowledges is primary to the narrative therapy interview). The privileging of specific cultural practices over others also acts to disqualify whole groups of people, who through their actions are viewed by the culture as "different." These groups, who may practice a different sexual or spiritual orientation, political belief, etc., can be categorized and marginalized as not normal and thereby are not afforded equal rights given to others considered by society as normal.

Arguments for the ascendancy of one idea or practice over another promote the rhetorical position that actual "truths" exist (Miller, 1993). Foucault (1980) wrote the following:

> There can be no possible exercise of power without certain economical discourses of truth that operates through and on the basis of this association. We are subjected to the production of truth through power and we cannot possibly exercise power except through the production of truth. (p. 73)

Foucault's perception differed from traditional perceptions of power, which regard it as negative (a top-down form of power). He claimed that power does not come from above, but rather from below (the subject), where cultural knowledge claims are internalized and produced (and reproduced) in every social interaction. It is, therefore, not exercised negatively from the outside, although negation and repression may be one of the effects.

For example, if you are attending a class or workshop in psychology, look around the room and witness how, for the most part, people are dressed in a similar fashion. Although no one has received a memo outlining a dress code, the majority of participants are not dressed in costumes or wearing formal wear or pajamas. How did they know? The people in the room are also fully equipped with similar cell and smart phones, iPods, and computers churning out e-mails. The use of these products has been taken up by the industrial, economic, and social context for mass practice reproduction.

A knowledge practice viewed as truth within a cultural discourse sets standards for the specifications of the individual, around which the individual shapes his or her life (Foucault, 1984a). Once an individual becomes integrated into society's discourse, certain cultural truths are assumed and privileged, thereby restraining the construction and acceptance of alternatives (Breggin & Breggin, 1997). To participate in these truths, certain less dominant, less scientific, or perhaps lesser accepted truths are subjugated. In a videotaped discussion I had with Michael White in May, 1991, in Adelaide, South Australia[19] on power relations, he suggested that if therapists restrict themselves to a classical analysis of power, what remains invisible are the many social forces and structural inequalities that are shaping of people's lives and relationships.

A harrowing example of how our society privileged the White man's account of written history over the aboriginal people's account is a sample of a power-through-knowledge practice that neglects the idea of structural inequalities. The history we learned in our North American and European schools through written, visual, and oral accounts were (obviously) biased accounts of history that were written into our mainstream texts by the victors (Ken Hardy, keynote address, Therapeutic Conversations Conference,[20] 2004, Toronto, Ontario, Canada). The losers' (those who lost the war/territory/culture/language) story of historical events occurring throughout the Americas were (and for the most part still remain) silenced and stricken from historical record (Makungu Akinyela, keynote address, Therapeutic Conversations Conference, 2005, Vancouver, British Columbia, Canada). The aftermath of this tragic history of obliteration (at the hands of colonial English, Spanish, and French power/knowledge) is one in which first-nation cultures across the Canadian and American landscape experience extraordinarily high rates of HIV and AIDS, diabetes, tuberculosis, incarceration, suicide, substance use, and so on—all ranking far above the national average.

---

[19] See this video conversation at http://www.narrativetherapy.tv.

[20] The Therapeutic Conversations Conference is the annual event organized by Yaletown Family Therapy and the Vancouver School for Narrative Therapy in Vancouver, British Columbia, Canada and is a rich resource for narrative therapy material at http://www.therapeuticconversations.com.

When Foucault described truths, he was not suggesting that an objective reality actually exists; rather, he was referring to those constructed ideas that are afforded a "truth status." These truths set the standards of normalization and have influence on how people shape their lives and view themselves (Szasz, 2001). In Canada, the cultural story of how women are viewed and valued is highlighted when statistically they as a group have far greater numbers of people living in poverty.

The primary subjugating effect of power through truth and truth through power is the specification and formation of individuality, and this in turn is a vehicle for power (Parker, 1989). Foucault suggested that the cultural construction of power is not repressive, but rather acts in such a way to subjugate other alternative knowledges. Foucault wrote the following: "One must remember that power is not an ensemble of mechanisms of negation, refusal, exclusion. But it produces effectively. It is likely that it produces right down to individuals themselves" (O'Farrell, 2005, p. 113). He proposed that persons become docile bodies and are conscripted into performances of meaning, which lend support to the proliferation of both global knowledges and techniques of power (Foucault, 1989). Foucault then stated that there are no global knowledges that can be universally accepted as truth.

Writing in one of his most acclaimed (in my opinion) papers on the construction of personal failure, Michael White (2002) critiqued traditional notions of power. He wrote that when considerations of power are raised in the context of therapeutic explorations, invariably a classical analysis of traditional power is called to mind. This classical analysis conceives that (a) power is appropriated by certain individuals and groups and (b) power is taken up by these individuals and groups according to exacting interests. This describes a power that is understood to exist at a defined center and that is exercised from the top down by those who have a monopoly on it. It is a power that is characterized as principally negative in its function; that is, it is a power that operates to oppress, repress, limit, prohibit, impose, and coerce. This is a power that people are mostly subject to, not one that people generally participate in the exercise of. In contemporary times, this version of power is often considered to be synonymous with the system ("the system") that virtually everyone is on the outside of. In situating their lives, people routinely claim a position that is exterior to this power, regardless of whatever privilege they might have on account of where their lives are located in the domains of class, race, economics, and social advantage (White, 2002).

White (through his close reading of Foucault) took issue with these prevailing ideas of power because he saw that the operations of power were dependent on people's active participation as its instruments (Michael White, personal conversation, 1991[21]). So despite the pervasiveness and effectiveness of power, individuals are uniquely placed to challenge and to subvert the operations of modern power. In challenging the dispositions and habits of life that are fashioned by modern power, people can play a part in denying this power its conditions of possibility (White, 2005).

## COMMUNITIES OF DISCOURSE

The list of right ways and wrong ways of living is lengthy. Some ideas are restrictive, some are liberating, and some may be viewed as disconnecting (Hoakwood, 1993). Each idea attempts to locate and compare us within the current normal human bell curve that tests, evaluates, and determines our personal worth. We ask ourselves if we are "in" or "out," or if we "fit in." Our complex relationship with our community of discourse, and the prevailing Western ideology supporting this discourse, shapes and influences how we believe we should and should not live our lives (Caplan & Cosgrove, 2004).

Our community of discourse (Madigan, 1992) is a cultural creation. Our community of discourse is not based in truth but does involve all the rules we make up in formulating what is believed to be normal and what is not. Our community of discourse allows for social norms to be dictated through a complex web of social interchange mediated through various forms of power relationships (Hare-Mustin & Maracek, 1995; Law & Madigan, 1994; Shotter, 1989; Shotter & Gergen, 1989; Spivac, 1996). The

---

[21] For more on this conversation on power relations, see my 1992 interview on http://www.narrative therapy.tv with Michael White.

community discourse we perform is not a neutral entity, because any discourse has potentially perverse effects on the lives of persons and problems within the community of its creators (Horkeimer & Adorno, 1972).

For example, the body mass index (BMI), which is expressed as a simple height–weight ratio, has replaced the old insurance tables as the universal gauge for "healthy" weight. The BMI "goalposts" were recast in 1998 by a team of medical doctors, resulting in millions of previously healthy people suddenly being redefined as overweight. Using this new measuring stick, a 6-ft man is considered overweight at 184 lb, obese at 221 lb, and morbidly obese at 295 lb. If you go by the current BMI, most North Americans in their 50s are too fat.

Another community of discourse is represented through the multidisciplinary team "chosen" to make decisions on what to include and exclude in the *DSM*. This particular dominant discourse showcases how a small professional group can produce enormous discursive influence in our community (Breggin, 1994a; Caplan, 1994). The *DSM* group is given the task of figuring out what and who is normal and what and who is not[22] (Caplan, 1991, 1995). The group does this by voting on the particularities of fixed categories of human life. For example, the *DSM* board of advisors has the power to decide whether to include hypoactive sexual desire disorder in this year's manual and whether to exclude caffeine-related disorder as a classification.

After the votes[23] are counted on classifications, professional communities take up the affirmed *DSM* constructions and reproduce them within their own various fields as if they were fact (e.g., in legal arguments, mental-status examinations, child-custody agreements). This reproduction of psychological theories takes place despite the fact that *DSM*-based research has repeatedly shown very poor reliability and, therefore, questionable validity. In a 2005 interview, Robert Spitzer, the architect of the *DSM*, confessed candidly, "To say that we've solved the reliability problem is just not true. It's

---

[22] White professional males have primarily constituted the dominant group responsible for the development of *DSM* nosology, deciding which behaviors are to be considered healthy and unhealthy (Caplan, 1995).

[23] The *DSM* is more a political document than a scientific one. Decisions regarding inclusion or exclusion of disorders are made by majority vote rather than by indisputable scientific data.

been improved. But if you're in a situation with a general clinician it's certainly not very good" (Zur & Nordmarken, 2007, p. 2).

The *DSM* outlines how our communities of discourse develop commonly held social constructions[24] of beliefs and truths. Overall, these internalized ways of knowing (Madigan, 2004; Parker, 2008) help us know when and if, for example, the music of the Irish rock band U2 or hip-hop music is still hip, whom to support among warring countries, and whether we should call people *patients, clients,* or just *persons.* The prevailing community discourse is often shaped by and shaping of numerous grand narratives such as capitalism, Judeo-Christianity, and the patriarchy (Armstrong, 1989; Jameson, 1991). Each narrative has its dissenters and its followers who constantly argue for and against an idea's legitimacy. But be it a matter of music or politics, wars are fought in the international, national, psychiatric, and family arena over which discourse holds the truth.

What constitutes our community of discourse includes a veritable potpourri of speakers. Discursive influences—including Sigmund Freud, CNN, NPR, the G8, and Karl Marx, as well as Jesus, Mohamed, Eli Lilly, Disney, the White House, and the United Nations. All are sculpted through intricate and ritualized power plays, and all are set up to control the discourse. All "knowing" within this community context is viewed as mutually shared and shaped (Madigan, 1996). Hence, I create you and you create me; governments shape us and we shape our governments.

Without exception, all conversations of our community that have gone before us are us, affect us, and are participated in by us. And because of the structure of our language (our use of nouns, verbs, and so on), persons cannot *not* take up rhetorical[25] positions, speaking or not speaking (Keeney, 1983; Tyler, 1986). Each generation of speakers—from the founding fathers

---

[24] Social constructionism and social constructivism are sociological theories of knowledge that consider how social phenomena develop in social contexts. Within constructionist thought, a *social construction* (social construct) is a concept or practice that is the creation (or artifact) of a particular group. Social constructs are generally understood to be the by-products of countless human choices rather than laws resulting from divine will or nature. Social constructionism is usually opposed to essentialism, which defines specific phenomena instead in terms of transhistorical essences independent of conscious beings that determine the categorical structure of reality.

[25] Emphasizing this close relationship between discourse and knowledge, contemporary rhetoricians have been associated with a number of philosophical and social scientific theories that see discourse as central to, rather than in conflict with, knowledge making.

of government to more current speakers such as the American Psychological Association, the National Association of Women, Greenpeace, punk musicians, and Apple computer's CEO—makes attempts to sway the discourse in particular directions and, of course, are swayed along, to and fro, by the discourse.

Michel Foucault (1965, 1980) suggested that within the process of knowledge acquisition, there are no truths about living, only interpretations of truth situated in rhetorical ethics (Goldstein, 1981; Madigan, 1992). Foucault claimed that all of our actions, from eating to dressing to working, are tied to and influenced by a specific community of prevailing discourse (Gutting, 1994). It would therefore be impossible to be situated outside the influence of one's culture and discourse or to believe that one's observations during a political debate and/or practice of therapy were neutral (Butler, 1997). And if we cannot escape these communities of discursive influence, we as narrative therapists are curious as to how they might relationally shape our relationship ecologies involving persons, problems, and the very practice of our therapy (Nylund, 2006b).

Narrative therapy perceives that whatever the discourse is that guides the therapeutic position we take in therapy, it is not neutral (Shotter, 1990a). Rather, the therapeutic positions we take are a response to cultural traditions, supported through political structures, and instituted through mental health systems (and other systems like medicine, science, the judiciary, and so on). This constitution of set institutionalized language rules affects our therapeutic language in every way (Bruyn, 1990; K. Gergen, 1991, 2009). For example, set mental health procedures and professional knowledge traditions determine who decides on the criteria regarding which individuals are invited to attend medical rounds and case conferences and, of those individuals, who is allowed to speak and what psychological ideas are privileged when addressing the client under review (Law & Madigan, 1994).

As therapists, we are required to be rigorously accountable and responsible for the choices we make when positioning ourselves among the countless variety of psychological models made available to us through a vast array of different mediums and institutions. The discourse involved in each distinct therapeutic dialogue can be viewed as the ideological stuff that shapes and influences a therapist's practice vision and wisdom[26] (Bakhtin, 1986; Freedman & Coombs, 1996; Madigan, 1991a).

## TEXTUAL DISCOURSE

Recognizing the community influence in our therapeutic theories, questions, meetings, and ways of constructing what we say in, for example, our case notes allows us as therapists the luxury of never having to view our therapeutic decisions as isolated or solitary. Rather, what we actually practice/write in therapy is shaped by myriad conversations situated within the vast terrain of cultural and countercultural learning and traditions (Madigan, 1991a). From a narrative therapy perspective, therapy practice is considered textual[27] discourse.[28]

For example, when working therapeutically with an indigenous person who views herself or himself as "less than worthy," the therapist might proceed to find an appropriate diagnosis and refer the person for medication and self-esteem groups. Alternatively, a narrative therapist might consider the therapeutic relationship to include a wider reaching context of the problem–person relationship (Freedman & Coombs, 2002). Taking this latter position on the problem (of less than worthiness), a narrative therapist might inquire about the relational and interactional means through which this person came to know herself or himself in this less-than-worthy way (Golan & White, 1995). Consideration might also be given to the indigenous person's experience with colonization, racism, multigenerational abuse, clergy abuse, and loss of belonging to their cultural language and heritage.

---

[26] I would suggest that if a therapist does not situate and recognize this community influence in therapy and/or the construction of problem making, the sociopolitical and cultural thrust of Epston and White's narrative therapy work will be lost (Madigan, 1996).

[27] Roland Barthes (in Madigan, 1991a) suggested that a culture and its texts should never be accepted in their given forms and traditions.

[28] I could go further and assert that the meaning of a text does not come into being until it is actively used in a context. This process of activation of a text by relating it to a context of use is what we call discourse. To put it differently, this contextualization of a text is actually the reader's (and in the case of spoken text, the hearer's) reconstruction of the writer's (or speaker's) intended message, that is, her or his communicative act or discourse.

When a therapist overlooks the relational "politics" of the problem–person context, he or she may find it difficult to separate the person from the problem in an effort toward re-storying. The political shaping of identity and the discursive practices supporting the person's identity context are of central importance to narrative therapy's idea of what helps to co-create therapeutic change.

## WHY DISCOURSE AND NOT LANGUAGE?

Discourses represent systematic and institutionalized ways of talking. Unlike language, discourse places emphasis on specific sets of actions or discursive practices rather than on abstract structures or processes (Anderson, 1990; Law & Madigan, 1994; Madigan, 1992). By inhabiting certain kinds of discourse, we commit to the existence of certain kinds of entities (e.g., a psychologist might begin to "witness" undifferentiated family boundaries, an overfunctioning mother, or high numbers of adolescents with attention-deficit disorder [ADD] from the same school district).

Discourse is viewed as both shaped by and shaping a sociopolitical context. The idea is described by social constructionist/psychologist Ken Gergen (1991) in the following passage:

> If our discourses are not derived from the facts, but once embraced they create what we take to be the factual world, then a more critical look at these discourses is in order. Because these discourses support and sustain various structures of power and privilege, certain people have been marginalized and oppressed by them. The critical literature seeks to demystify the voice of authority, and to increase the range of voices in the sanctuaries of power. (p. 96)

Michel Foucault (1984b) suggested that *discourse* refers not only to the actual words and statements themselves but to their connection with the complexities of social and power relations, which prevail in any given context and constrain what is said. Discourse spoken in this manner refers to both what can be said and thought, as well as who can speak and with what authority (Foucault 1994b; Parker, 1998). These recursive dimensions of discourse contain all forms of relational talk, including the talk of governments, academic institutions, therapy, the hospital ward, and the family.

From this poststructural perspective, meaning results not from language itself, but rather from institutionalized discursive practices that constrain and shape its use and that preempt alternative uses and meanings (M. White, personal communication, 1992). Hence, discourse can be viewed as reflecting a prevailing structure of social and power relationships that are actively constitutive in relationships (Michael White, personal communiction, 1990). In a sense, we are cospeaking ourselves into existence by inhabiting, mobilizing, and performing prevailing cultural discourses (Bakhtin, 1986; Nylund, 2004c; Turner, 1986).

For Foucault, subjectivity is a production of discourse as the self is subjected to discourse (Parker, 1989, 2008). For example, the way in which a client speaks about the meaning of his or her "primary" relationship is created within the cultural boundaries of how we have been trained up and consequently coproduce our view of relationships. Foucault took the position that what is considered to be in the realm of discourse is constitutive of the discourse (Parker, 1989, 2008). He wrote that what can be spoken about and who can speak it are issues of power relations. For example, who gets to make up the general rules surrounding the protocol on where a therapy session takes place, for how long, and who gets invited brings this issue into question.

Discourse has suggested that there are no foundational or structural realities to be discovered (Foucault, 1994b). Therefore, no claim to knowledge or truth has any grounding, except within the rhetorical terms of an institutionalized discourse (Rosen, 1987). To discuss psychology from this perspective encourages the address of psychology discourses and not psychological models or paradigms. Narrative therapy explains the stories told in therapy by confirming that there are no essences, only discourse (Law & Madigan, 1994).

British social constructionist/psychologist John Shotter (1990b) wrote that our major prosthetic device through which we can make contact and see others around us is discourse. Yet, the world of the modern structural/psychological/scientific traditions insists on seeing utterances as though sentences were pictures that represent the reality (Wittgenstein, 1953). Modernist/structuralist perspectives view the structure of the sentence as the things it represents, and this can be misleading for therapists in many ways. For example, Wittgenstein (1953, 1960) suggested that a way of speaking is what prevents us from seeing the "facts" (i.e., our practices and procedures of usage) without prejudice. In terms of discourse, those who support modernist/structuralist thought have implied that the individual and the external environment are the products of, rather than the sources of, discourse and signification[29] (Derrida, 1991).

The advocates of structuralism have also suggested that behavior reflects the structure of the mind (M. White, personal communication, 1997). For example, in the field of anthropology, we find the champion of the structuralist movement in Levi Strauss. By way of a simple explanation, his field work looked at two different cultures, and what he found was that their ceremonies were similar. His conclusion from this study of cross-cultural ceremonies was that because there was a similarity in ritual, each culture shared the same structural representations of the brain.

Similarly, within a variety of our counseling practices (e.g., family of origin, cognitive behavioral, psychoanalysis) there rests a foundational perception that in each person a surface behavior exists (Breggin & Breggin, 1994; K. Gergen, 2009). And beneath this layer of external behavior, the probing psychologist will hypothesize, ruminate, and eventually "find" the person's systems of deeper meaning. What the client says is viewed as content and what the therapist reads and interprets of this content is viewed as a preferred meaning known as *process.* Poststructuralists disagree.

Poststructural theory directs attention away from content-process language and toward discourse. According to English psychologist Rom Harre (Davies & Harre, 1990), discourse both historicizes and politicizes the study of language use. Unlike language, discourse places emphasis on specific sets of actions or discursive practices and not on abstract struc-

---

[29] Saussure offered a dyadic or two-part model of the sign. He defined a sign as being composed of a "signifier" (*signifiant*)—the *form* that the sign takes, and the "signified" (*signifié*)—the *concept* it represents.

tures or processes (Rose, 1989). This view of discourse is associated with postmodernism and poststructuralism (and particularly the work of Michel Foucault; e.g., Foucault, 1979, 1980, 1984a, 1984b) in that discourse is viewed to express the historical specificity of what is said and what remains unsaid (Tyler, 1990).

Davies and Harre (1990) also suggested that to know anything is to know it in terms of one or more discourses. By inhabiting a particular discourse, we become more committed to the existence of certain kinds of entities and to the acceptance of certain statements as true. American philosopher Richard Rorty (1979) wrote that as we begin to move along the spectrum from habit to inquiry, the acquisition of "attitudes towards new truth-value candidates" (p. 94) are introduced. To inhabit a discourse is like laying out a semantic path in front of us as we talk, where typically we have the illusion that it was already there waiting for us and that it was the natural and obvious path to take. These truth-value candidates act as other alternative beliefs that can be woven into the fabric of the reweaving process of re-authoring (Epston & White, 1992).

Narrative therapists support the idea that discourse represents all institutionalized ways of talking (Jenkins, 2009; Nylund, 2004b, 2006a; Reynolds, 2010; Sanders, 1998). This institutionalization of talk occurs across all levels of social, political, cultural, psychological, and family discourse. Specific discourse of various kinds are produced and lobbied for, and they have continued to evolve throughout history (Parker, 2008; Sampson, 1993). Examples of these include the discourse specific to a wide variety of psychological beliefs and to all other landscapes of talk. This includes talk as diverse as the talk of sports (Nylund, 2007a), substance use (Sanders, 1998), attention-deficit/hyperactivity disorder (ADHD; Law & Madigan, 1994), dance (H. Nanning, personal communication, 2009), HIV and AIDS (E. Mills, personal communication, 2007), ideology and education (P. Orlowski, personal communication, 2003), art (D.O'Connor, personal communication, 2010), politics (Jameson, 1991), music (A. Cash, personal communication, 2002), social activism (V. Reynolds, 2004), film (N. Jordan, personal communication, 2000 and literary theory (Eagleton, 1991).

These differing talk formulas are said to be performed,[30] and they compete with each other to produce distinct and incompatible versions of reality in which no one specific landscape of talk is viewed as separate or unique, as all are joined within the culture's discourse (Madigan, 1997). Shotter (1989) wrote that a speaker's failure to take into account those certain other considerations of standpoint has the effect of maintaining a system of beliefs.

Typically, the beliefs maintained are those of the status quo (and specific) privileged (discourse) within specified landscapes of power, knowledge, and rhetoric. He considers this lack of consideration as an error of method because all matter of conversation and investigation must be open to correction of error (i.e., scientific experiments, religious belief, therapeutic diagnostics). But very often, objections to the dominant frame of thought are either rendered unintelligible or assimilated in some way.

## IDEOLOGY NOT EPISTEMOLOGY

Derrida (1991) wrote that the subject can never be set apart from the multiple others who are its very essence. He brings forth the important distinction between the terms *ideology* and *epistemology* (when referring to the study of how ideas/meanings are generated). The theories of ideology highlight the link between social ideas and politics, power, and practices (Eagleton, 1991). Theories of epistemology concentrate on suppositions inherent to inquiry, including the relations among ideas, observations, and explanation.

This distinction points out a crucial factor absent in the metatheoretical debates and practice orientations within our field of psychology (Nylund, 2004a). What appears to be missing from the discussion is the investigation of how epistemological decisions are shaped by ideological commitments (Kearney & Rainwater, 1996).

---

[30] Victor Turner (1986) suggested that performance has become a popular signifier expanding the definitions and assumptions of a range of social phenomenon. The power of the idea is captured when we think of human beings as a performing species. Turner suggested that rather than see ourselves as *Homo sapiens*, we would be better served to see ourselves as *Homo performas*. If we accept this, performance therefore becomes necessary to our survival.

Ideological punctuations are not evenly honored as social contexts arise in specific historical circumstances that legitimate certain meanings while obscuring others (Madsen, 2007). For example, a pledge to an ideology of equal opportunity may occur in a patriarchal social organization, but the meaning of equality is tempered by ideas of fairness—a term itself with a history shaped by the patriarchal context and representing an unequal play of power (Goldstein, 1981).

White and Epston (1990) spoke about ideology in this way:

> Our preferences for some analogies over others are multi-determined, including by *ideological factors and by cultural practices.* In privileging one analogy over another, we cannot resort to criteria such as correctness or accuracy, since such attributes cannot be established for any analogy. However, we can, at least to an extent, investigate the analogies through which we live *by situating our own practices* within the history of social thought and by examining and critiquing the effects of these practices. (p. 5)

In summary, ideologies cannot be viewed as arbitrary punctuations because they reproduce relations of power that are legitimized by numerous cultural institutions.

## NARRATIVE'S PROBLEM LOCATION OF THE "I"

Key to moving Epston and White from a structural to poststructural view of therapy was a commitment to "retool" the central tenets of mental health language (McLeod, 2004; White, 1997). Of central concern was the need to address the relational context between the person and the problem.

Narrative therapist Johnella Bird (2000, 2004) of Auckland, New Zealand, wrote about the challenge of addressing the issue of the word *I* in mental health language. She perceived that the conventions of English language usage locate experiences within people (clients; e.g., "I'm sad"). In this example, the languaging practice ("I'm sad") acts to encourage the speaker and the listener to consider that sadness exists within the body of *I*. In other words, if we language the problem and find its place of origin inside the

"I"/self, then the body of the person will be the point of origin the therapist sets out to "fix."

Bird (2000, 2004) suggested that the problem with mental health language is that static representation of experience has severe consequences for those people (clients) who are struggling with life experiences and circumstance. Conventional English language strategies create the conditions in which the *I* is seen, experienced, known, and/or captured as autonomous, self-directed, singular, and independent.[31]

Many fields of social science have struggled to situate the "I" outside the body and within a relational, discursive context (Taylor, 1989). As far back as the 1930s, Russian psychologist and linguist Mikhail Bakhtin (1986) argued that

> neutral dictionary definitions of the words of a language ensure their common features and guarantee that all speakers of a given language will understand one another, but the use of the words in live speech communication is *always* individual and contextual in nature . . . the word is expressive, but, this expression does not inhere in the word itself. (p. 88)

John Shotter (personal communication, October 1991) suggested that a word's meaning (in this case the word *I*) does not inhere the word itself, but originates at the point of contact between the words used and the movements they achieve in the condition of their use.[32]

Therefore, the words we use in therapy to describe exactly who clients "are" are not neutral or isolated (Crapanzano, 1990). Rather, the words we use are situated in discursive contexts and connected within relationships of present and prevailing professional power and knowledge.

For example, narrative therapy would not perceive the use of the word describing the problem of anorexia as inherent to the person suffering (i.e.,

---

[31] It is important to note that whenever we use the English language conventionally in our clinical work, we unwittingly support conversational processes that persistently subject people (clients) to "self" and "other" evaluation, categorization and diagnosis.

[32] It is here at this point, the point at which Clarke and Holquist (1984) so aptly called "the combat zone of the world" (p. 307), that Shotter (1990) suggested our struggle over the question of the speaker's rights and privileges (compared with those of the listener) takes place.

that girl is anorexic; Borden, 2007; Grieves, 1998; Madigan & Epston, 1995; Madigan & Goldner, 1998; Maisel, Epston, & Borden, 2004; Nylund, 2002a; Tinker & Ramer, 1983). Rather, the person suffering would be viewed within a complex discursive relationship with anorexia—a relationship defined by all those contributing aspects of our culture viewed as supporting of the performance of anorexia (Gremillion, 2003). Narrative therapy practice would not support any wide sweeping attempts in psychological research to explain anorexia within a biological explanation (that tries to locate anorexia inside the frontal lobe of a person's brain). Nor would narrative therapy embrace any of the million-dollar research projects that look for the elusive anorexic gene (which, more than likely, is hiding beside that still-elusive alcohol gene). For the narrative practitioner, a person's relationship to anorexia is situated within the socio-political-cultural domain of community discourse (Madigan & Goldner, 1998).

From a narrative therapy perspective, anorexia is viewed, in part, as a response to a postcapitalist engendered body politic (Bordo, 1989, 1993). In other words, the person's relationship to anorexia is but one means of responding to the demands of the culture that the person is currently living within (Diamond & Quinby, 1988). This particular relational expression, responded to through the body, is viewed as a reply to culture and the vast regime of gender expectations and perfection training demanded of women (and more and more men).

Narrative therapy locates anorexia within a discursive culture and not inside the private isolation of the person's body. A narrative therapist questions the popular community discourse surrounding anorexia and studies the process of how and through what means mental health invented anorexia as a pathology to be placed inside the bodies of the women afflicted. Narrative therapy supports the idea that the person did not invent the practices associated with anorexia on his or her own (this also supports a belief that the emotional, medical, and financial burden of anorexia should not placed onto the solitary back of the person who is struggling; Dickerson & Zimmerman, 1992; Madigan & Goldner, 1998).

Despite the obvious correlational social shaping of the problem of anorexia, the prevailing treatment for those struggling with eating disorders places the primary therapeutic focus on the individual's relationship with food ("Shari," personal communication, 2003, Vancouver Anti-Anorexia/Bulimia League and weight (Grieves, 1998; Madigan, 1996; Madigan & Goldner, 1998), as well as on what the professional states about the individual's mental health (Gremillion, 2003). These professionally dominant ideas that influence eating disorder treatment are supported through the communities discourse about anorexia—even though the professional discourse often divides the subject off from any contextual explanation or investigation into the communities of discourse supporting of anorexia.

Being exposed to this line of treatment, the person is afforded little exploratory time for a much broader investigation into the taken-for-granted cultural tyrannies of thinness, ongoing surveillance of the body, perfection training, gender training, and why so many persons in the culture are feeling that they are less than worthy, out of control, and not quite measuring up (D. Epston, personal communication, 1991).

## RAINBOWS OF DISCOURSE

With a little knowledge of discourse, poststructuralism, and identity politics, a narrative therapist operates within the relational dialogues and discursive influences that are shaping the therapeutic session. Because of the many discursive influences that have an effect on who we are and how we practice our lives (K. Gergen, 1989, 2009), a therapist is not merely having conversations with single solitary individuals and/or families in a neutral conversational space (Madigan, 1996, 2007, 2008; Nylund, 2002a, 2003).

A therapist is in conversation with a variety of discourses ("sitting" alongside a variety of similar and different other discourses) that have helped clients toward certain ideas about who they are in relationship to themselves, the culture, and others (White, 1991). We are, therefore, never alone with the persons who come to see us in our therapy office—as we (client and therapist) are heavily populated by many sets of mobile discourses.

To help illustrate this point, we might consider a quick look at a rainbow. From my layperson's perspective, a rainbow is a relationship of colors, light, and space in which the relationship of all colors, light, and space are directly affected through a relationship of recursion; simply put, everything is affecting everything else within a specified context (like the snake eating its tail).

Despite this system of complex interaction, we continue to look up to the sky and state, "Oh look at that lovely shade of green in the rainbow"— we believe we are seeing only the single band of green, but we are actually viewing the color green interacting with the blurring of a color spectrum (the influence of blues and yellows on the green), the pollution context, our physical position in relation to the rainbow, and our social constructions of rainbows, color, and so forth.

This fixing of green into space gives us the illusion of a single color unaffected by the physical and constructive context; however, we do not really see green. We see only a blurring of a colored context as we temporarily allow ourselves and others the luxury of separating the green out from its relational spectrum. To map this rainbow metaphor onto a particular problem in therapy (e.g., Little Johnny's overfidgeting at school), a therapist might get caught up in constructing the particulars of the problem in the same way that we believe we see the color green in the rainbow. Taking this particular clinical position on the fidgeting problem is in concert with popular, albeit modernist, practice ideology.

The difficulty with the modernist position of seeing green is our forgetting to put the green back into the context of the rainbow and surrounding environment. Hence, overfidgeting little Johnny is often treated as an isolated strip (Goffman, 1961) and set apart from the relational, linguistic, political, and experiential context. Having worked with a lot of overfidgeting "Johnnys," I know that what often precedes the visit to see me is the following: Johnny's body is professionally read, inscribed, and privatized with the problem and labeled accordingly within the widely accepted belief in the individualized pathology of ADD or ADHD. This untested theory and vast overusage of the ADD and ADHD diagnosis (Breggin, 1994; Nylund, 2000, 2002b), and the subsequent chemical restraints that flow from our theories onto millions of little Johnny's bodies, is more often than not a clear example of therapists seeing green as separate from the rainbow's context.

A larger relational context involving education policy, school-board funding, dual-parent work schedules, latch-key kids, overcrowded classrooms, underpaid teachers, increased violence and fear in the schools, sugar-based diets, lack of sleep and exercise, and so on, are worthy considerations of Johnny's contextual rainbow.

## CONSTRUCTING "REALITIES"

French deconstructionist Jacques Derrida (1991) suggested that the speaker can only speak from a set of preexisting frames or preunderstandings. In other words, our utterances are shaped through a scaffolding of presuppositions (Madigan, 1991a); that is, what we know in our lived experience is shaped through the cultural weave of community discourse. For example, therapists who train within schools of psychiatry, psychology, and social work or within cognitive–behavioral or psychodynamic therapy are "shaped" in the way in which they come to see and talk about problems, families, couples, and individuals.

Hans-Georg Gadamer wrote that we cannot step over our shadows (Moules, 2007). He suggested that people are connected in a continuous thread with their past, with traditions, and with their ancestors. This is not an epistemological quest because we are historical beings, living out traditions that have been bequeathed to us by others. And although we may be taking up traditions in many different ways, they are still the source of who we are and how we shape and live our lives. The echoes of this history are inadvertently and deliberately inviting us into both past and new ways of being in the present. We live in a world that recedes into the past and extends into the future, so rather than pitting ourselves against history, we need to remember, recollect, and recall it. The address of tradition is not just something arching from before, for we are in tradition (Moules, 2007).

Therefore, each and every encounter a therapist has is under the influence of his or her pretraining in life (e.g., family, school, country, culture, race, class, sexuality, gender). We can change the specifics of the relational presuppositions we live through, but we can never fully escape their restraints (Bateson, 1979; Watzlawick, 1984) to be completely free of our history and tradition of presuppositions. It is the interpretive strategies of the interpreter who points us toward the situated knowledge of the therapist, as this situated knowledge mediates the semantic intent of our therapeutic conversations (i.e., what Michael White's co-construction of "sneaky poo" was, and what this co-construction means to the client or another therapist looking on is something very different.

Narrative therapy places the site of the problem within the relational action of person/culture/discourse/power and, as a result, not inside the person's body. A narrative approach to problems is isomorphic to the golden rule of real estate buying: location, location, location! When narrative therapists take the poststructural step not to privatize problems inside a person's body, then the person, problem, and therapeutic resolutions begin to look relationally quite different.

Epston and White's separating the person from the problem (Epston, 1988) is by no means a trivial step, as it paradigmatically shifts the therapist and client outside the realm of 150 years of psychological "science." For example, much of what we are taught in graduate school, along with what we read, speak, and practice inside the domain of mental health, is from an individualizing perspective—a perspective that situates the site of the self and the problem inside the body of the person (Madigan, 1999). Johnella Bird (2000) wrote that "a relational conversation shifts linguistically what has been or what is subjectified (i.e., attributes, ideas, feelings, experiences that are conceptualized as belonging to the person) to the status of an object in relationship to the person (client)" (p. 43).

The therapeutic act of respecting the tenets of relational languaging shifts the focus away from the individual self to a self always in relationship (Caplan, 1984). Therefore the *I* as we know it never stands on its own. The *I* is related to and known, experienced, and located as (always) being in the situated context of a relationship.[33]

---

[33] To further our understanding of this paradigm shift, it is important to embrace a narrative difference, because (as the English/American scholar Gregory Bateson was fond of saying), "it is the difference that makes the difference." To consider preparing yourself for a journey of difference, it might be wise to suspend a "comparative" practice view regarding what you have already learned in graduate school and professional practice. So if you find yourself thinking at any time during the reading of this book something like "Wow, this sounds a lot like Professor Smith's lecture on CBT" or "It's just like the training I did in motivational interviewing," you'll need to realize that you've just left the poststructural field we are traveling in.

# DISCURSIVE IDENTITY

"Identity," said feminist Jill Johnston, is "what you can say you are, according to what they say you can be" (Foucault, 1989, p. 71). The identity she is referring to is not a freely created product of introspection or the unproblematic reflection of a private inner self (Spivak, 1996). The dominant Western understanding of identity is based in great measure on a liberal individualist framework, which is maintained and shaped through the institutions, discourse, and archives of science (Law & Madigan, 1994).

Since the 17th century, science has owned the study of the body. Psychiatry, psychology, and other helping professions, such as social work and family therapy, have welded themselves onto to this scientific project and appropriated their slice of its proprietorship. For these disciplines of (pseudo)science to obtain "title" to the body has required that the body's meaning be rendered utterly transparent and accessible to the qualified specialist (assisted by the proper methodology and technology) and adequately opaque to the client and his or her community of supporting others.

From a narrative therapy standpoint, the concept of identity is cultural, discursive, multisited, multistoried, contextual, and relational. Narrative therapy considers identity not as "one's own," as characterized by the Enlightenment's creation and production of the self-contained individual and its search for a singular, unifying fundamental governing principle. The alternative view that narrative practice supports is that any identity will build on its relations to other identities so that nothing can be itself without taking into consideration the kinds of relationship by which the "selfsameness" is constituted (Sampson, 1993).

Narrative practice organizes around the idea that identities are conceived within certain dialogic, ideological frameworks constructed by the dominant social order as the vehicle to maintain special interests (M. M. Gergen & Gergen, 1984). For example, specific and long-standing religious conceptions regarding the identity and status of women are illustrations of the dominant male group securing its beliefs and interests in the social ordering of life. In turn, women take up and perform these male-dominated constructions of their identities or face the cultural consequences if they resist (see Caplan, 1995). For example, a few hundred years ago, tens of thousands of women were once deemed evil and threatening to the virginal men operating the Catholic Church. The threat was performed into meaning when women were constructed as witches, then murdered through a variety of heinous methods by those carrying out the orders of the church.

Identities and our remembrances of our identities are profoundly political both in their origins and in their implications (Madigan 1993a, 1993b, 1996). Our distributed and negotiated selves (K. Tomm, personal communication, 1986), and the selves we normally remember, are influenced by and reproductive of cultural and institutional norms. As contributing members of this community of identity and discourse, we come to experience ourselves within the relational politics of these dominant norms (are we in or are we out, are we normal or abnormal, do we measure up or down, and are we acceptable worthy citizens, parents, workers, lovers, and so on).

Poststructuralists argue for a consideration of a posthumanist and decentered view of identity (Butler 1997; Hoagwood 1993; Huyssen, 1990). This position unsettles any essentialist psychological notion of the stable autonomous person, the original author (of problem conversations or otherwise), or a given reality of what constitutes the self (Spivak, 1996).

According to the turn of the century Russian psychologist Vygotsky (Daniels & Wertsch, 2007), all higher order mental processes exist twice: once in the relevant group, influenced by culture and history, and then in the mind of the individual. Therefore, the development of the person is dependent as much on interpersonal relations as it is on individual maturation.[34] Vygotsky was arguing back in the late 1920s and early 1930s that all learning was social. His theories were in direct contradiction with the dominant theories on child development of the day (offering a difference to developmental theorists like Piaget). Vygotsky's (1978) famous passage states:

> Every function in the child's cultural development appears twice: first,
> on the social level, and later, on the individual level; first between

---

[34] Michael White suggested that Vygotsky called that place where we provide therapeutic conversations for people to cross over the gap (from the known and familiar to the what might be possible to know) the "Zone of Proximal Development" (M. White, personal conversation, 2004).

people (interpsychological) and then inside the child (intrapsychological). This applies equally to voluntary attention, to logical memory, and to the formation of concepts. All the higher functions originate as actual relationships between individuals. (p. 57)

During the early 1930s, Mikhail Bakhtin, who was a Russian psychologist and linguist, suggested that we are direct contributors to each other's identity. Bakhtin described a relational view of the self when he stated that "[I] get a self that I can see, that I can understand and use, by clothing my otherwise invisible (incomprehensible, unutilizable) self in the completing categories I appropriate from the other's image of me (Clark & Holquist, 1984, p. 79). Bakhtin's belief is that the other plays a central role in constituting the individual's self. And without the ongoing relationship to the other, our selves would be invisible, incomprehensible, and unusable. The other gives us meaning and a comprehension of our self so that we might possibly function in the social world (Liapunov & Holquist, 1993). The knowledge we have of ourselves appears in and through social practices— namely, interaction, dialogue, and conversation with others' responses.[35]

Bakhtin wrote that we

> address our own acts (addressive quality) in anticipation of the responses of real others with whom we are currently involved; imagined others, including characters from whom we are currently involved; historical others, including characters from our own past as well as from cultural narratives; and the generalized other, typically carried in the language forms by which a given community organizes its perceptions and understandings of its members, which we have learned to employ in reflecting us back to us. (Sampson, 1993, p. 106)

We are therefore equal contributors to each other's emerging identity.

From this perspective, the problems that people encounter can be situated within a dialogic context and not placed under individual sovereignty. Within narrative therapy's mode of practice, problem-saturated

---

[35] These interactions do not make us passive, nor are the discourses without a rhetoric of intent (Billig, 1990; Sampson, 1993).

stories in our lives are seen to gain their dominance at the expense of more preferred, alternative, or subordinate stories that are often located in marginalized discourses. This marginalized discourse is a form of knowledge and practice often disqualified or "invisibilized" by discourses that have gained hegemonic prominence through their acceptance as guiding cultural narratives (Spivak, 1996). Examples of these subjugating and normalizing narratives include capitalism, communism, psychiatry/psychology, patriarchy, Christianity, heteronormativity,[36] and Eurocentricity.

In addition, commonly accepted binary descriptors such as healthy/ unhealthy, normal/abnormal, and functional/dysfunctional ignore both the complexity of peoples' lived experiences as well as the personal and cultural meanings that may be ascribed to their experiences within a given context (see Foucault, 1965, 1994a, 1994b; Madigan, 1992, 1996, 2007; Madigan & Law, 1998; Nylund, 2007b; Nylund, Tilsen, & Grieves, 2007; Tilsen & Nylund, 2008, 2009). For example (see Madigan, 2008),

> central to many psychotherapeutic services is the dual process of documenting client lives and relationships through naming (who the client is) and writing practices. How and what we identify and document is organized through set institutional, political, and economic structures. (p. 89)

Central to our culture's dominant humanist psychology movement is the idea of self-determination and growth through an independent transcendence of the self (Spivak, 1996). Foucault suggested that this would be difficult to achieve because all our actions, from eating to dressing to working, are tied to and influenced through our prevailing normative cultural discourse.

In a parallel critique of humanism, narrative therapist Michael White (1997) considered the essentialism underlying humanist conceptions of the identified self in therapeutic culture to be quite "limiting." White (1997,

---

[36] *Heteronormativity* is a term for a set of lifestyle norms that indicate or imply that (a) people fall into only one of two distinct and complementary sexes (male and female) with each having certain natural roles in life, and that (b) heterosexuality is the only normal sexual orientation, thus making sexual and marital relations appropriate only between members of the opposite sex. Consequently, a heteronormative view is one that promotes alignment of biological sex, gender identity, and gender roles to the gender binary.

2004, 2007) stated that he did not believe the practice of narrative therapy is "a recycled structuralist/humanist psychological practice" that involves "discourses of psychological emancipation." He posited that narrative therapy is not a "libratory approach that assists persons to challenge and overturn the forces of repression so they can become free to be "who they really are" so that they can identify their "authenticity" and give true expression to this (White, 1997, p. 217). Narrative therapy offers the person a relational context to view himself or herself and the problem from multiple perspectives.

Narrative therapy does not view a person as fixed within problem identities; a person's identity is viewed within the politics and power plays of a culturally manufactured and constituted self (Foucault, 1973, 1977; M. White, personal communication, 2004). For example, if a sole-parent woman of color and mother of two children under the age of 3 who is living on social assistance has been referred to therapy to discuss her anxiety by a social worker, the discussion does not center on how she can improve herself and stop the anxiety. In this woman's case, any narrative therapy discussion about the problem that did not include the politics of gender, race, and poverty would be viewed as unethical.

In the future, there will be many new and evolving theoretical issues and social movements that are bound to influence narrative therapy. As narrative theory moves forward, a few ideas will remain consistent to its practice of therapy, such as anti-individualism, a consideration of power relations and structural inequalities, listening to voices in marginalized places, and appreciating the wonder and imagination of how persons respond to our culture (Tilsen & Nylund, 2009).

# 4

# The Therapy Process

*The real political task in a society such as ours is to criticize the workings*
*of institutions that appear to be both neutral and independent, to criticize*
*and attack them in such a manner that the political violence that has*
*always exercised itself obscurely through them will be unmasked,*
*so that one can fight against them.*

—Michel Foucault (*The Chomsky-Foucault Debate: On Human Nature*)

Oliva Espin (1995), Professor Emerita of women's studies at San Diego
State University, has critiqued most traditional forms of therapy as
a result of being primarily informed by essentialism and the treatment of
scientifically verifiable disorders. Espin has suggested that modernist/
scientific therapies have been particularly harmful to clients of color,
believing that they are often pathologized because of not living up to

---

Portions of this chapter have been excerpted or adapted from handouts created by Stephen Madigan for use
in his workshops at the Therapeutic Conversations conferences. Some material in this chapter reprinted from
"Anticipating Hope Within Conversational Domains of Despair," by S. Madigan, 2008, in I. McCarthy and
J. Sheehan (Eds.), *Hope and Despair in Narrative and Family Therapy*, pp. 100–112. Copyright 2008 by
Bruner Mazel, London. Reprinted with permission.

White, universal norms of behavior (Nylund, 2006a). According to Espin, many therapies inadvertently reproduce racist discourses. Espin (1995) stated that

> a social constructionist paradigm that sees psychological characteristics as a result of social and historical processes, not as natural, essential characteristics of one or another group of people is the more productive approach in the study of diversity than some other traditional paradigms accepted in psychology. (pp.132–133)

For White and Epston (1990), therapists are "inevitably engaged in a political activity in the sense that they must continually challenge the techniques that subjugate persons to a dominant ideology" (p. 29). Narrative therapist David Nylund (2006a) suggested that therapists must always assume that they are producing in domains of power and knowledge and operating within systems of social control.

## JESSIE'S STORY

I met with Jessie, an 11-year-old African American boy, in Chicago as part of a narrative therapy consultation, demonstration, and narrative therapy training video (as a result of geography, I only had one therapy session with Jessie and his African American mother). Prior to our meeting, I was told that Jessie had been recently suspended from school for assaulting a White male peer from his class (Carlson & Kjos, 1999). The school principal, the classmate's parent, and a counselor had supported sending him to court. The court had then ruled that he receive court-ordered therapy for anger management. According to both Jessie and his mother, the suspension and required therapy were unfair because the White child involved in the assault had hit Jessie first, and it was perceived by both children that neither "hit was a hit to hurt." Jessie's White classmate had not received a suspension or any other reprimand for his part in the interaction.

Jessie was sent to counseling by the juvenile court system. When I asked his mother why she thought they had come to see me, she answered that she "didn't think he needed counseling but just a good talking to."

When we explored the conversation further, she let me know that her son Jessie was sent to court because of a claim initiated by the White mother of the student he had exchanged "hits" with. Jessie explained to me that these were not "hits to hurt," but rather "fooling around kinds of hits." He also stated that when they got back to class from the bathroom where the fooling around kind of hits happened, he and his classmate had laughed together.

As the interview unfolded, Jessie's mother told me that not only had her son been suspended from school, but when he went to court he was charged with battery, placed on 1-year probation, given 40 hours of community service work, and levied a $300 fine. Jessie's mother said that she believed the "White judge treated Jessie as if he knew him."

After the court proceedings ended, the mother of the White student apologized to Jessie's mother because of the "harsh" sentencing. The other mother had apparently initiated the court proceedings against Jessie with the understanding that he would just get a "slap on the wrist." Had Jessie been White, the White mother's understanding of legal events may have proven correct, and she may not have needed to apologize. Jessie's mother stated that she hoped that the other student's mother had learned the hard lesson that not all people are treated equally in the courts. Without this understanding, Jessie suffered at the hands of the White mother's privileged "not knowing" internalized racist position.

Throughout the course of our 1-hour session, I became curious as to how the issue of race might have influenced how Jessie was being viewed and subsequently treated. It was my understanding that Jessie was not in need of anger management counseling (and this was good because I don't know how to "do" anger management counseling, nor am I interested in doing it). As an alternative, I began to introduce narrative therapy questions around the topic of internalized racism as a possible way to locate, understand, and explain Jessie's predicament. Being the person with power and privilege in the session, it was up to me to broach the issue of race with the hope that Jessie's mother felt safe enough to discuss it with me (K. Hardy, personal communication, 2004). I have outlined below a small fragment of our discursive interaction.

**Madigan:** [addressing Jessie's mother] Do you think race had something to do with how Jessie was treated?

**Mother:** I think so because if it had been a White boy, it was a White boy, but if it had been two White boys, I don't think they wouldn't have went to court.

**Madigan:** Are you saying that the other child involved with Jessie was White?

**Mother:** Yes. He was, he's not a bad boy, either, it's just that the parents, both of them just made a big thing out of it.

**Madigan:** As a mother, how does it feel to have Jessie exposed to this legal and education system where he might get treated differently because of the color of his skin?

**Mother:** Well, I don't like it.

**Madigan:** What part of this do you most not like?

**Mother:** Well, I've been told that this new school has not gotten use to having Black kids—so they have to be real careful.

As the conversation continued, I began to deconstruct the racist social practice of labeling African American male youth as *deviant, conduct disordered,* and/or *criminal.*

**Madigan:** [asking the mother] Do you think that trouble [the problem that was relationally externalized] might find the African American children in the school quicker and they'll unfairly develop reputations of trouble more than the White children in the school?

**Mother:** Yes, I think so.

**Madigan:** [later in the session] Do you have any final words you'd like to say?

**Mother:** I'd like to say I didn't know we would get to tell this story but it's a true story.

**Madigan:** And I just want to tell you that I really believe your story. And I'd like to stand behind your story in any way that I can. And I am very sad that this story is going on for you.

**Mother:** Yeah, me too.

**Madigan:** I'm saying that as a person here with you, and I'm also saying that as a White person. Thank you so much for coming and sharing this story with us.

**Mother:** Okay. Thank you so much.

After the session, I wrote a letter to the school principal outlining my questions and concerns regarding the treatment Jessie received by the school, its counselor, and the judiciary system (see Exhibit 4.1). My primary apprehension was how Jessie would be written up into a file as a dangerous and violent student—and how this file would not only follow him but have long-reaching negative effects on his reputation and his future social and academic career.

I also took time after our session to recruit members of Jessie's community into a different telling of who he was as a person by writing them a therapeutic letter (see Exhibit 4.2). My hope in writing this letter to them was to create a counterfile that was supportive of Jessie's good-boy reputation.

The therapeutic story of Jessie and his mother (see Exhibit 4.3) outlines how problems are often inscribed onto individuals through generalized taken-for-granted ideas—in this case, generalizing by the school, parents, judges, psychology, and the probation system regarding the reputation and character of Jessie. This kind of common psychological "branding" action took Jessie and his family to a powerfully punishing place, where a more relational and contextual rendering of ideas regarding how people are constructed may have spared this family some pain. How this 11-year-old African American boy came to be described, disciplined, and punished had a strong relationship to our community's dominant ideas about people—in this case, an African American youth. These ideas about Jessie were constructed and shaped by dominant ideas, taken-for-granted notions, and disciplinary measures, which were then shoved onto his identity/body.

Narrative therapy practice is premised on the notion that people organize their lives through stories (thus the use of the narrative or text metaphor). When a client comes to talk with us, he or she usually relates a telling of his or her life through stories (Dickerson, 2009). Clients tell these stories by linking their understanding of the problem, relationship,

## Exhibit 4.1    Letter Sent to the School Principal

Dear Mr. _____:

My name is Dr. Stephen Madigan. I am a family therapist who had the pleasure of talking with one of your students, Jessie_____, and his mother last week.

The reason I am writing is to discuss my concerns regarding the school's participation in events this past fall that have placed Jessie's reputation as a good student, friend, and son in a certain kind of danger. To begin with, it is very clear to me that Jessie does not need anger management treatment.

My primary concern at this time is Jessie's future reputation as a student in your school program. My fear is that the fugitive reputation the court has given him is unjust and that this unjust reputation will be written into his school file. I fear this because it has been documented that Jessie was charged with battery, placed on probation, and given a hefty fine along with 40 hours of community service work. I am concerned how this negative documentation of Jessie will negatively affect how his teachers, classmates, and your administration interact with and treat him. I am also concerned about how this negative reputation might affect Jessie's view of himself.

As a principal, you have certainly experienced how difficult it can be for some students to live down a bad reputation. Jessie has done little to deserve the harsh personal and financial punishment he received, and I believe that other factors such as race, social status, and class may have influenced his sentence.

I would appreciate a time set aside to talk to you about these concerns.

Sincerely,

Stephen Madigan, MSW, MSc, PhD

## Exhibit 4.2    Letter Sent to Jessie's Group of Supporters

Hello. My name is Dr. Stephen Madigan, and I am a family therapist who is working alongside Jessie and his mother. I am writing to ask for your support and share some ideas regarding an unfortunate legal matter Jessie has encountered.

Jessie and his mother were sent by the juvenile justice system to me for anger management counseling. It quickly became apparent to me that something awfully wrong had happened to Jessie, and as a result, his hard-earned reputation as a good student, friend, and son was in jeopardy.

Did you know that because of an admitted "fooling around kind of hit" between him and another student, Jessie was forced to go to court? He was then levied a hefty fine, probation, and community-work hours. Did you know that the young White classmate's mother has apologized for setting up Jessie's court appearance because she believed that he would merely get a "slap on the wrist?" Did you know that the judge treated him, in Jessie's mother's words, "like he already knew him?"

Jessie and his mother have let me know that the school he attends has "not yet gotten used to having African American children in their classrooms." I wonder what you make of this? And I wonder if you believe this had any influence on how he was treated at school and in the courts?

My concern is that through this unfortunate legal experience, Jessie might be forever viewed as a violent offender, a person not to be trusted, and a negative student.

As all of you probably realize, Jessie does not deserve the fugitive reputation the school and legal system have now given him. I am

*(continued)*

> ## Exhibit 4.2 Letter Sent to Jessie's Group of Supporters (*Continued*)
>
> writing to ask your support in helping us reclaim his real reputation as a good and hard-working student/son/friend and stand against this bad-person reputation.
>
> If it is possible, I am asking you to write a letter on Jessie's behalf that stands in support of him. I am asking you to include a description of your experience of him, what he means to you as a person, and what future you see Jessie being able to embrace.
>
> You can send the letters to Jessie at _____.
>
> Thank you for your help in this matter.
>
> Warmest regards,
>
> Stephen, Jessie, and his Mother

illness, and so on, through a sequencing of life events and ideas through time (J. Bruner, 1990). People often speak about what brought them into therapy, what they believe the history of their situation is, and who or what is responsible. At the time that someone decides to come to therapy, there is usually one prevailing theory told as to what they are in therapy for, and this theory is often thought to be quite limiting of their descriptions of themselves and their situation.

Narrative therapy practice is based on the idea that people make meaning in the world about who they are—and who they are in relation to others—through a dialogic relationship that is considered shaped by the prevailing cultural group. To offer a more colorful snapshot of their lives, clients' stories introduce a range of characters and "back" stories in just the same way that any good author's stories might. Although people live and construct stories about themselves, these stories also live and construct people (Bakhtin, 1986; J. Bruner, 1991; K. Gergen, 2009; Parker,

---

**Exhibit 4.3    Return Letter From Jessie and His Mother**

The following letter was sent 4 weeks after our counseling session.

Dear Mr. Stephen:

Thanks a whole lot for helping us. We got loads of sweet letters about my son. Jessie reads them and feels good and so do I.

My pastor and friends in our church and the social worker and a few neighbors met with Jessie's principal and teacher. It was some meeting and we think that everyone now feels sorry for what happened to Jessie a little while ago. The principal said he knows what a good child he is and this made us both feel real good. Our pastor gave the principal what for, and he told the principal to write to the judge, but who knows if anything will happen.

Jessie says he will never do anything bad at school again and says that his teacher is being nice to him and he got four perfect marks on four different tests. He said his teacher thinks he is smarter than most of the other kids.

Thanks that you paid the money to the courts for us.

I hope you come and visit.

Jessie's Proud Mother!

---

2008; White, 1995a). If, for example, from a very young age a person from a marginalized group is given the message that somehow he or she is a less-than citizen, how that person performs his or her life as a citizen will be under the influence of the dominant and accepted construction of who the person is viewed to be, as set forth by the prevailing cultural group (K. Hardy, personal communication, 1998; Tilsen & Nylund, 2009; see also Hardy, 2004; White, 1987, 1988).

The narrative therapist holds a firm belief that the person arriving into therapy is not solely responsible for creating the problem-centered, deficit-identity conclusion that the person often relates to us. For example, mothers experiencing a child viewed by the preschool as "not quite fitting in" (what might be considered "proper" preschool behavior) may blame themselves as being unfit (following in step with a predominance of mother-blaming ideas in our culture; Freeman, Epston, & Lobivits, 1997). Young girls struggling with body perfection feel they have personally failed (Dickerson, 2004); a heterosexual corporate employee not able to spend more time with his or her children feels socially torn and inadequate (D. Grigg, personal communication, 2007); a gay or bi-curious high school student is entered into a fearful secrecy and feels a sense of individual shame (D. Nylund & J. Tilsen, personal communication, 2006).

The ensuing story told by these persons in therapy is often one that adheres to specific "individual responsibility" for "their" problem and a desperate desire to be "fixed." This perplexing humanist notion of individual responsibility for the daily problems we collectively create, experience, and reproduce appears cut off from the relational context of prevailing cultural.

A belief that a person does not measure up to cultural expectations can quite easily discount the alternative skills, competencies, beliefs, values, commitments, and abilities that the person has achieved (as a means of living/surviving within the parameters of dominant norms). It is within the process of re-authoring the larger multistoried cultural context of personhood that therapist and client begin to guide their discussions away from individualized problem stories and toward richer and thicker (Geertz, 1983) narratives (emerging out from under the initial problem-based disparate descriptions of experience; White, 2005).

Narrative therapy interviewing is based on the person's storied accounts regarding his or her experiences and actions in life (Nylund & Hoyt, 1997; White, 1987). Narrative therapists are not concerned with behavior, as in categories of behavior. Instead, they turn their attention toward action and interaction—that is to say, the action and interaction of experience, response, and reflection of the client. Within the practice of narrative therapy, problems are viewed as relational, contextual, interpretive, and situated within dominant discourse, expression, response, and cultural norms. This interplay presents the backdrop to the narrative maxim—the person is the person, and the problem is the problem—not separate but culturally, discursively, and relationally interwoven.

## RE-AUTHORING CONVERSATIONS

Re-authoring conversations[1] (White & Epston, 1990) is a key feature of the practice of narrative therapy. Re-authoring conversations invites clients to help flush out some of the more neglected areas and events of their lives (often covered over by the problem story being told). These may include achievements under duress; survival skills growing up; and personal qualities left out of their story, such as generosity, ethical stances, and kindness. These are very often stories that could not have been predicted through a telling of the dominant problem story. These untold stories can be sadly neglected in the telling of the problem story by both client and the professionals involved with the client's story.

Neglected events in the client's life are viewed as exceptions or unique outcomes[2] that are used as a beginning point for re-authoring conversations and the development of alternative story lines. Often these conversations evoke a longer standing curiosity and appreciation about the story the clients find themselves telling. The telling of these alternative and often preferred recollections of their lives and relationships shapes newly formed stories that can be further broadened and enriched (Hall, McLean, & White, 1994).

Narrative therapists ask questions as a way to expand on the alternative or subordinate story by trafficking in what Jerome Bruner (1990, 1991) called the *landscape of action* and the *landscape of identity*.[3] Landscape of

---

[1] For an excellent resource on re-authoring conversations, read Michael White's (1995) text, *Re-Authoring Lives: Interviews and Essays*.

[2] For a more in-depth discussion on unique outcomes, I recommend Epston's (1988) *Collected Papers* and White's (1989) *Selected Papers*, published through Dulwich Centre Publications.

[3] For a more in-depth discussion on Bruner's landscape of identity and landscape of identity questions, please refer to J. Bruner (1990) and White and Epston (1990).

action questions center on events that happened in a person's telling of his or her life and links these events through time, forming a plot line. These questions are organized through events, circumstance, sequence, time, and plot (M. White, personal communication, 1991). Landscape of identity questions are (in part) those that are asked regarding what the client might conclude about the action, sequences, and themes described in response to the landscape of action questions. Landscape of identity questions also bring forth relevant categories that address cultural identities, intentional understandings, learnings, and realizations.

Taken together, the landscape of action and landscape of identity questions assist in re-authoring client lives and relationships by listening in to find the sparkling undergrowth and unique outcomes through the client's understanding of events. Therapists take a full accounting of who was involved in the creation of the problem story, how the person came to know himself or herself in this problematic way, the life-support systems of the problem, the possible losses involved in his or her life and relationships in relation to the problem, any resistance that the person has noticed regarding his or her response to the loss, and what all these events mean to the person telling the story.[4]

During the first therapeutic conversation, the person coming to therapy usually becomes involved with the narrative therapist in two separate descriptions: (a) a problem-saturated story line and (b) an alternative plot to the problem story (that lies alongside and is often preferred). In developing this scaffold of curiosity and questions, narrative therapists traffic in (a) landscape of action questions (composing events linked in sequence; through time; and according to the who, what, and where of the story) and (b) landscape of identity questions (composing identity conclusions that are shaped by contemporary identity categories of culture— the person's conclusions about the story; J. Bruner, 1990; Winslade & Monk, 2007).

---

[4] Refer to Madigan's workshop handouts, Therapeutic Conversations Conference, http://www.therapeutic-conversations.com.

People's stories of life and of personal identity can be considered to compose landscapes of the mind (M. White, personal communication, 1992) that are constituted through landscapes of action and landscapes of identity. It is through narrative therapy questions that these alternative landscapes of the mind can be richly described and re-authored.

Re-authoring conversations act to reinvigorate a client's sense and meaning of the story by highlighting the gaps and refined understandings of this information. This newly recollected information results in a change within the problem-saturated story being told. Questions continue to unearth an archive of relevant and preferred local information about the client's abilities, hopes, dreams, and commitments. The conversation shifts from one of a bored and overtold rendition of the story toward a fresh and vibrant retelling—complete with stories of competencies, agency, and knowledge.

Combining the different landscapes, narrative therapy acts to

- question how the "known" and remembered problem identity of a person has been influenced, manufactured, and maintained over time;
- question what aspects of the social order have assisted in the ongoing maintenance of this remembered problem self;
- locate those cultural apparatuses keeping this remembered problem self restrained from remembering alternative accounts and experiences of lived experience;
- locate alternative sites of resistance through questioning how the person can begin to re-remember subordinate stories of identity living outside the cultural, professional, and problem's version of them;
- influence how discursive space can afford room for possibilities and different discursive practices to emerge by resisting and standing up for the performance of this re-remembered and preferred self; and
- explore who else in the person's life might be engaged to offer accounts of re-remembrance and provide the person safety within the membership of a community of concern (Madigan & Epston, 1995).

For example, narrative therapy might pose a question about the construction of men's lives to a man or group of men who have come to therapy. A therapist might ask them what term they might use to describe the essential aspects of masculinity and what it means to be a man. We could pose the following questions:[5]

- What are the practices of life and ways of thinking about life that stand behind this word/term (that they have described regarding being a man)?
- Are their certain requirements and ways that you live because of this particular way of thinking?
- What are these ways of living (practices)?
- How do these ways of living, etc., have you relating to yourself?
- Do they bring you closer in or further away (to yourself or others)?
- Are there any downsides to living this way of thinking for your relationships with others? For yourself?
- In what specific ways do these ideas (practices) about being a man shape your life?
- If you had to (or if you were to decide to) step further along this way of living, what do you imagine this would require you to do to your life in the future?
- From another person's perspective, what would appear to be for you and against you in taking up this lifestyle?
- Do you have any thoughts on at what point in the history of men's development as men these essential ideas about being a man first emerged?
- What did these ideas make possible and what did they limit?
- Can you identify the exact ways in which you were drafted into these particular men's ways of being?
- Was it worth it or not worth it to give your life over to these ideas?

A narrative therapist might then ask the men to reflect on just one occasion in their lives when they found themselves standing outside the taken-for-granted thinking about being a man. The men might be asked the following questions: What do you picture in yourself that leads to your

---

[5] The following questions have been influenced through the work of Alan Jenkins and Michael White.

taking this step? How did you prepare yourself for this step? What other developments were taking place in your life at this time that may have been related to this step you took? Would you consider this a giant step or a little step? Why? How did you approach this step? Was it ever touch-and-go for you? Who else can you think of that may have contributed to this step? At what point did you begin to realize that you had stepped toward something different and significant?

Once a history of ideas past and present has been established, a narrative therapist would continue with the line of questions:

- What does this tell you about how you wish your life to be?
- What does it say about you as a parent/partner/lover that stands in good favor to you?
- Thinking back now, can you recall any other events that have happened in your life that might reflect your preference for these steps and ways of living?
- What can you tell me to help me understand the bedrock ideas these steps are imbued in?
- How did these earlier events shape your values in terms of the relationships you have with women and children in the present?
- Whose specific reactions to these events most reflect these values and beliefs for you?
- Will these knowledges and experience in any way affect your responses to sexism, men's violence, or perhaps gender inequalities?

Moving along in our conversations with this group of men, a narrative therapist might recognize that it's one thing to have these versions of whom we might be in relation to other ways of being with women and children, but it is another thing to have the practices and the know-how to bring these thoughts into action. We might ask the following questions:

- What experiences provoked these thoughts?
- And what were these thoughts exactly about?
- Were there specific important people in your life who contributed to these ideas as possibilities?

- In what ways did they contribute?
- Did they offer you some substitute ways of being with women and children that you might have favored?
- At what point in your life did you step into these other ways of being?
- How did you develop the know-how that was required to accomplish this?
- Did you achieve this primarily through trial and error?
- If so, who provided the feedback to you along the way?
- Who were the people who provided you with examples of living in your preferred ways?
- Did they provide you with some sort of guidebook?
- If so, how did you find yourself entering into these practices?
- What do you imagine they might say about their contribution that you've taken up?
- If you were to go further toward these other ways of being a man, where do you think it might take you?

## RELATIVE INFLUENCE QUESTIONS

From the outset of our narrative therapy history, the therapeutic interview involved relational externalizing, unique outcomes, unique accounts, unique possibilities, unique redescription,[6] and unique circulation questions, as well as experience of experience, preference, and historical questions.

Everyday narrative therapy interviewing involves a process known as *relative influence* questioning, which comprises three sets of questions: (a) One set maps the influence of the problem on the person and losses experienced within this relationship, (b) another set encourages persons to map their own (and others') influence in the life of the problem (White,

---

[6] As a sampling of how questions help in the re-authoring of people's lives, Michael White (1988) wrote that unique re-description questions assist in the revision of persons' relationship to themselves (e.g., In what way do you think these discoveries could affect your attitude towards yourself?), with others (e.g., How might this discovery affect your relationship with . . . ?), and with problems (e.g., In refusing to cooperate with the problem in this way, are you supporting it or undermining it?).

1988), and (c) the third set begins to map out the unique outcomes or the occasions in which the person experienced some influence in his or her life despite the discursive power of the problem.

Woven together, relative influence questions invite a re-telling of the client story in such a way as to evoke a discursive means of understanding and performing aspects of the client's abilities and skills in the face of the problem (Nylund & Thomas, 1997). Below is the frame and structure of a narrative therapy interview that I learned in my apprenticeship and ongoing relationship with David Epston and Michael White (a relationship that continues in many parts of the world and is intentionally practiced at the Vancouver School for Narrative Therapy).

## Mapping the Influence of the Problem in the Person/Family's Life and Relationships

How does the problem influence the person(s) life, relationships, and loss?[7] Mapping the problem's influence on the person/relationship helps to mutually develop an understanding of the experience-near, problem-saturated story.

It is crucial for the therapist to take enough time to develop this line of inquiry for persons to feel their experience is "known" and for them to "know it" in a way that offers them a different, more detailed perspective on the problem's effects on their lives and relationships and their response to this relationship. Often I will track and question the losses that have occurred in the person's life while in relationship to the problem. For example, people in long-standing relationships with drugs, anorexia, anxiety, and so on, will always report losses concerning relationships with friends, school, jobs, hobbies, and family.

An expansive mapping at this stage of therapy opens multiple opportunities for exploring unique outcomes later. It also gives a rich sampling

---

[7] Some material in this section is adapted from *Framework for a White/Epston Type Interview*, by S. Roth and D. Epston, and retrieved from http://www.narrativeapproaches.com/narrative%20papers%20folder/white_interview.htm. Copyright 1995 by the Dulwich Centre. Adapted with permission.

of people's language habits (Madigan, 2004) around the problem. Questions to ask may include the following:

- How does worry feature in your work life? In your life beyond work? In your relationships?
- When worry is having its way with you, what happens to your dreams for the future?
- Are you satisfied or dissatisfied with the way the worry is (as you stated) "wrecking my relationship" and leaving you no time for friends?
- What dissatisfies you the most about worry's relationship to you and your relationships?

## Mapping the Influence of the Person/Family in the Life of the Problem

Through mapping the influence of how people may be problem supporting, clients can begin to see themselves as authors, or at least coauthors, of their own stories. They can then move toward a greater sense of agency in their lives as primary author of the story to be told and lived through. A broad mapping at this stage opens multiple opportunities for exploring unique outcomes later. It also gives a rich sampling of people's language habits (Madigan, 2004) around the problem. Questions to ask may include the following:

- Are there ways in which you have unknowingly given worry the upper hand in your life?
- Have there been people or situations in your life that have helped you keep worry central to your life?

## UNIQUE OUTCOME QUESTIONS

Unique outcome questions invite people to notice actions and intentions that contradict the dominant problem story. These can predate the session, occur within the session itself, or happen in the future.

- Given over-responsibility's encouragement of worry, have there been any times when you have been able to rebel against it and satisfy some of your other desires? Did this bring you despair or pleasure? Why?
- Have there been times when you have thought—even for a moment—that you might step out of worry's prison? What did this landscape free of worry look like?
- I was wondering if you had to give worry the slip in order to come to the session here today?
- What do you think it may have been that helped support the hope in yourself that helped you sidestep worry?
- Can you imagine a time in the future that you might defy worry and give yourself a bit of a break?

## UNIQUE ACCOUNT QUESTIONS

Conversations develop more fully following the identification of unique outcomes and begin to demonstrate how they can become features in a preferred alternative story. Unique account questions invite people to make sense of exceptions/alternatives to the dominant story of the problem being told (e.g., I always worry). These exceptions may not be registered as significant or interesting or different; however, once uttered and uncovered, they are held alongside the problem story as part of an emerging and coherent alternative narrative.

Unique account questions/answers use a grammar of agency and locate any unique outcome in its historical frame, and any unique outcome is linked in some coherent way to a history of struggle/protest/resistance to oppression by the problem or an altered relationship with the problem.

- How were you able to get yourself to school and thereby defy worries that want to keep you to themselves at home alone?
- Given everything that worry has got going for it, how did you object to its pushing you around?
- How might you stand up to worry's pressure to get you worried again, to refuse its requirements of you?

- Was it easier to be worry free for those moments when you were simply watching that movie unencumbered?
- Could your coming here today be considered a form of radical disobedience to worry?

## UNIQUE RE-DESCRIPTION QUESTIONS

Unique re-description questions invite people to develop meaning from the unique accounts they have identified as they re-describe themselves, others, and their relationships.

- What does this tell you about yourself that you otherwise would not have known?
- By affording yourself some enjoyment, do you think in any way that you are becoming a more enjoyable person?
- Of all the people in your life who might confirm this newly developing picture of yourself as worrying less, who might have noticed this first?
- Who would support this new development in your life as a worry-free person?
- Who would you most want to notice?

## UNIQUE POSSIBILITY QUESTIONS

Unique possibility questions are viewed as next-step questions. These questions invite people to speculate about the personal and relational futures that derive from their unique accounts and unique re-descriptions of themselves in relation to the problem.

- Where do you think you will go next now that you have embarked on having a little fun and taking a couple of little risks in your life?
- Is this a direction you see yourself taking in the days/weeks/years to come?
- Do you think it is likely that this might revive your flagging relationship, restore your friendships, or renew your vitality? (This conversation can lead back to unique re-description questions.)

# UNIQUE CIRCULATION QUESTIONS

Circulation of the beginning preferred story involves the inclusion of others. Circulating the new story is very important because it fastens down and continues the development of the alternative story (Tomm, 1989).

- Is there anyone you would like to tell about this new direction you are taking?
- Who would you guess would be most pleased to learn about these latest developments in your life?
- Who do you think would be most excited to learn of these new developments?
- Would you be willing to put them in the picture?

## Experience of Experience Questions

Experience of experience questions invite people to be an audience to their own story by seeing themselves, in their unique accounts, through the eyes of others.

- What do you think I am appreciating about you as I hear how you have been leaving worry behind and have recently taken up with a bit of fun and risk?
- What do you think this indicates to Hilda (her or his best woman friend) about the significance of the steps you have taken in your new direction?

## Questions That Historicize Unique Outcomes

These questions represent any important type of experience of experience questions. Historical accounts of unique outcome allow for a new set of questions to be asked about the historical context. These questions serve to (a) develop the blossoming alternative story, (b) establish the new story as having a memorable history, and (c) increase the likelihood of the story being carried forward into the future. The responses to these produce histories of the alternative present (M. White, personal communication, 1993).

- Of all the people who have known you over the years, who would be least surprised that you have been able to take this step?
- Of the people who knew you growing up, who would have been most likely to predict that you would find a way to get yourself free of worry?
- What would "X" have seen you doing that would have encouraged him or her to predict that you would be able to take this step?
- What qualities would "X" have credited you with that would have led him or her to not be surprised that you have been able to_____?[8]

## PREFERENCE QUESTIONS

Preference questions are asked all throughout the interview. It is important to intersperse many of the previous questions with preference questions to allow persons to evaluate their responses. This should influence the therapist's further questions and check against the therapist's preferences overtaking the client's preferences.

- Is this your preference for the best way for you to live or not? Why?
- Do you see it as a good or a bad thing for you? Why?
- Do you consider this to your advantage and to the disadvantage of the problem or to the problem's advantage and to your disadvantage? Why?

## CONSULTING YOUR CONSULTANTS QUESTIONS

Consulting your consultants questions serve to shift the status of a person from client to consultant. The insider knowledge the person has in relationship to his or her experience with the problem—because of lived experience—is viewed by the therapist as unique and special knowledge. The insider knowledge is documented and can be made available to others struggling with similar issues (Madigan & Epston, 1995).

- Given your expertise in the life-devouring ways of anorexia, what have you learned about its practices that you might want to warn others about?

---

[8]Once the therapist begins to get a grasp on the format and the conceptual frame for developing temporal questions (past, present, or future), unique account questions, unique re-description questions, etc., they become a easier to develop and will eventually seem "ordinary" to the interviewer and the context.

- As a veteran of anti-anorexia and all that the experience has taught you, what counterpractices of fun and risk would you recommend to other people struggling with anorexia?

The structure of the narrative interview is built through questions that encourage people to fill in the gaps of the alternative story (untold through a repeating of the problem-saturated story). The discursive structure assists people to account for their lived experience, exercise imagination, and circulate the remembered stories as meaning-making resources.

The therapeutic process of narrative therapy engages the person's fascination and curiosity. As a result, the alternative story lines of people's lives are thickened (Turner, 1986) and more deeply rooted in history (i.e., the gaps are filled, and these story lines can be clearly named).

## COUNTERVIEWING QUESTIONS

Personally, I only ask questions in therapy, or at least I ask questions 99% of the time.[9] This is the way I was taught by David Epston and Michael White and the way that has always felt the most comfortable.

For the experienced narrative therapist, questions are not viewed as a transparent medium of otherwise unproblematic communication. It is considered a common practice for narrative therapists to be deeply committed to the ongoing investigation and location of therapeutic questions within community discourse as a way of figuring out the history and location of where our questions come from (Madigan, 1991a, 1993a, 2007). The process of discovering the influences that shape therapeutic questions and discussing why we use them with the people we talk with in therapy is viewed as a practice of therapist accountability[10] (Madigan, 1991b, 1992). Questioning therapists about their therapeutic questions is also used as a framework for narrative supervision (Madigan, 1991a).

---

[9] I created the idea of counterviewing questions as a means to explore and explain the deconstructive method involved in narrative therapy interviewing.

[10] For further reading on accountability practices, see Hall, Mclean, and White (1994) and Tamasese and Waldegrave (1994), *Dulwich Centre Newsletter*, Nos. 1 and 2.

Experiencing a close-up re-reading of therapy allows the idea of counterviewing questions (Madigan, 2004, 2007) to emerge. A narrative therapy organized around counterviewing questions speaks to narratives therapy's deconstructive therapeutic act. Narrative questions are designed to both respectfully and critically raise suspicions about prevailing problem stories while undermining the modernist, humanist, and individualizing psychological project.[11]

Narrative therapy counterviewing also creates therapeutic conditions to do the following:

- explore and contradict client/problem experience and internalized problem discourse through lines of questions designed to unhinge the finalized talk of repetitive problem dialogues and create more relational and contextual dialogues,
- situate acts of resistance and unique accounts that could not be readily accounted for within the story being told,
- render curious how people could account for these differences,
- appreciate and acknowledge these as acts of cultural resistance, and
- rebuild communities of concern.

Narrative therapy's method of close-up deconstructive counterviewing engages the relational world of therapeutic interviewing in the following ways:

- Counterviewing is an intensely critical mode of reading professional systems of meaning and unraveling the ways these systems work to dominate and name.
- Counterviewing views all written professional texts (files) about the client as ways to lure the therapist into taking certain ideas about the person for granted and into privileging certain ways of knowing and being over others.
- Counterviewing is an unraveling of professional and cultural works through a kind of antimethod that resists a prescription—it looks for

---

[11] For a clear example of counterviewing, see the American Psychological Association six-part DVD live session set of Stephen Madigan's narrative therapy work, *Narrative Therapy Over Time* (2010).

how a problem is produced and reproduced rather than wanting to pin it down and say this is really what it is.

- Counterviewing looks for ways in which our understanding and room for movement is limited by the lines of persuasion operating in discourse.
- Counterviewing also leads us to explore the ways in which our own therapeutic understandings of problems are located in discourse.
- Counterviewing allows us to reflect on how we make and remake our lives through moral-political projects embedded in a sense of justice rather than in a given psychiatric diagnosis.

## COUNTERVIEWING AND NARRATIVE THERAPY: THE ISSUE OF RESPECT

Counterviewing in narrative therapy is profoundly respectful. The method attempts to (a) "do justice" to the stories people tell about their distress, (b) respect the experience they have with the problems of living, (c) appreciate the struggles they are embarking on, and (d) value and document how they have responded to the problem.

The therapist's task is to work within these descriptions and acknowledge the complexity of the story being told so that contradictions can be opened up and used to bring forth something different (by sustained reflection), moving toward a "sparkling undergrowth" needing attention (White, 1997). Noting a story's contradictions allows for the elaboration of competing perspectives as the person's story unravels. These different competing perspectives seem to lie side by side and fit together, but there is a tension between them as they seem to try and make us see the world in different ways at one time.

A one-perspective story holds the person in the grip of the problem's/ professional's point of view. Against this professional standpoint is the perspective that flows from the client, who is simultaneously trying to find ways of shaking the problem and perhaps escaping a branded diagnostic name altogether. To be respectful to the differing viewpoints does not mean abandoning our own standpoint, but it does mean acknowledging where we stand.

## COUNTERVIEWING AND NARRATIVE THERAPY: THE ISSUE OF CRITIQUE

Counterviewing in narrative therapy is intensely critical of many therapy practices that are embedded in images of the self and others and that systematically mislead us as to the nature of problems. Narrative practice does not presuppose a self, which lies "under the surface" as it were. Counterviewing also alerts us to the ways that dominant ideas of the self get smuggled into therapy under the disguise of helping others.

Dominant narratives of mental distress can all too quickly lock us back into the problem at the very moment we think we have found a way out. The task of a counterviewing therapist, client, and interview is to locate problems in (cultural) discursive practices in order to comprehend how patterns of power/knowledge[12] provide people with the idea that they alone are to blame for these problems, they are helpless to do anything about these problems, and they should not maintain much hope (Madigan, 2008). In counterviewing practices, change is seen to occur when we are working collaboratively through the spaces of resistance that are opened up and made available by the competing accounts and alternative practices. It is here that hope may rise again.

## INTERNALIZED CONVERSATIONAL PROBLEM HABITS

My fascination with the specific workings of internalized conversational problem habits first began in 1993, when David Epston mentioned that he had interviewed young women from around the world who were struggling with relationships to anorexia and bulimia. He observed that even though the women's accents (e.g., English, French, Spanish, Swedish) were

---

[12] Michael White (1995a, 1995b) wrote that "since the pathologizing discourses are cloaked in impressive language that establishes claims to an objective reality, these discourses make it possible for mental health professional to avoid facing the real effects of, or the consequences of, these ways of speaking about and acting towards those people who consult them. If our work has to do with subjecting person's to the 'truth' then this renders invisible to us the consequences of how we speak to people about their lives, and of how we structure out interactions with them; this mantle of 'truth' makes it possible for us to avoid reflecting on the implications of our constructions and of our therapeutic interactions in regard to the shaping of people's lives" (p. 115).

very different from one another, their descriptions of the internalized habitual language[13] of anorexia and bulimia were almost identical. This brought me to the shores of a frightening conclusion: The language, practice, rules, and rituals of eating disorders were being exported worldwide! I was stunned to witness and realize how fast a proanorexic discourse was traveling through different cultures.

From these realizations, we began a more thorough investigation into Foucault's writings on Jeremy Bentham's design and creation of the Panopticon, along with Foucault's ideas on power/knowledge, subjectification, and internalized cultural discourse. We began to investigate (in therapy) what the discursive apparatus was regarding how these internalized cultural dialogues worked, where they came from, what supported their injurious linguistic life, and the ways they perform our lives. At the Vancouver School for Narrative Therapy, we started a project to map out exactly what the internalized problem habits were saying and how we were responding.

In our close-up study and documentation of the internalized discourse of problems, I began to realize that, from the cradle, we learn our culture codes through imitation—we copy what we watch and hear. It is ritual observance. We learn from those who learned before us how to walk, brush our teeth, ride a bicycle, spell words, speak language, and adhere to ethics and good manners. We fashion our talk and ways we perform and see the world through an internalized fragmented "karaoke" form of the others—while they are doing the same. We sing their songs of right and wrong and catalog this in cultural verse. Within the generative discursive space of our living world, narrative possibility was not restricted nor restrained to exclude the multiplicity and fusion of alternative rhymes and reason (Madigan, 2004; Nylund & Ceske, 1997).

Through a close reading of our session transcripts, it appeared to us that, as citizens, we partake in a practice of ongoing internalized conversations with ourselves (and imagined others) as a way of measuring ourselves against the external world, trying to determine if we fit in and are acceptable

---

[13] See Madigan's (2004) work on internalized chitter-chatter. A book titled *Chitter-Chatter—The 8 Conversational Habits of Highly Effective Problems* is currently being written for the public. The text is an anti–self-help book to promote ideas supporting poststructural mental health ideas for the masses.

and wondering if we are "normal" (i.e., normal parent, employee, partner, and so on). These internalized conversations are a mediated discourse of what is currently considered normal living/being through standards set by prevailing cultural ideas. As citizens, we perform, reproduce, and respond to these prevailing ideas and sculpt our lives—en masse—accordingly.

Through David Epston's influence, I began spending more close-up ethnographic co-research time with insiders with their knowledge about problem conversations, particularly members of Vancouver's Anti-Anorexia/Bulimia League. What was eventually co-researched and encountered were eight primary injurious conversational habits:[14] (a) self-surveillance/audience, (b) illegitimacy, (c) fear, (d) negative imagination/invidious comparison, (e) internalized bickering, (f) guilt, (g) hopelessness, and (h) perfection. Following is a brief review of what the therapeutic co-research into internalized conversational habits found.[15]

## Self-Surveillance/Audience

A quick summation of our earlier discussion on Michel Foucault's third mode of objectification analyzes the ways in which human beings turn themselves into subjects (Madigan, 1992), which he identified as *subjectification* (Foucault, 1965, 1983). Subjectification involves those processes of self-formation in which the person is active. Foucault was primarily concerned with isolating those techniques through which people initiate their own active self-formation. Foucault contended that this self-formation has a long and complicated history as it takes place through a variety of operations on people's own bodies, thoughts, and conduct (Foucault, 1980). These operations characteristically entail a process of self-understanding through internalized dialogue mediated through external cultural norms. Foucault (1973) suggested that people monitor and conduct themselves according to their interpretation of these set cultural norms. He viewed the process of internalized personal discourse—the conversations we internal-

---

[14]I suppose one could make a very good argument to include anger, mistrust, blame, shame, and countless other internalized problem conversations, and they would be absolutely correct in their assessment.

[15]What is often relationally externalized in narrative therapeutic conversations are the eight internalized problem conversations, the cultural chitter-chatter conversations we inhabit.

ize from culture to ourselves—as an action of self-control guided by set social standards. This seems to be why inhabitants within each distinct culture appear to know a specified moral code reflected within performed themes of living and located within their own present culture (Madigan, 1999, 2003; Nylund, 2007a).

Within this recursive/discursive frame, it is often only negative knowledge that supports the problem's version of the person.[16] Internalized self-surveillance and the thoughts of the negative-perceiving audience are present in the struggles with any problem because without an internalized act of self-surveillance and a dialogic injurious audience of support, a problem cannot survive. Problems often develop when we encounter an "I think that you think that I think" (that I am a bad person, partner, son, etc.) and so on, supporting a negative imagination internalized conversation of the other looking on to our experience.

Following are some counterviewing questions to consider:

- What constitutes an audience/spokesperson?
- What does the chitter-chatter conversation say?
- How does it work?
- By what means is the surveillance audience supported?
- Who is involved in this specific problem audience?
- What/who constitutes the you-supporting alternative audience?
- What are the major discursive influences affecting your internal self-surveillance system?
- When is self-surveillance most self-supporting?

Imagine the following scenario: You are a professional hired to work in the field of mental health. You have just suffered through a terrible divorce. The negative thrust and audience to this internalized story may involve many institutions and individuals. It involves negative conversations about the deficit "you" across the temporal plain and with persons both dead and alive. The internalized negative-observing self-surveillant/audience

---

[16] British psychiatrist R. D. Laing wrote about something similar in his fascinating book of interactional poetry *Knots*, and I believe it was Harry Stack Sullivan who wrote about the issue of projective identification—their fascinating ideas, however, neglected the poststructural community dialogic component of situating problem talk within dominant discourses.

opinions that the habit can draw from may include the surmised negative view of you from the legal team, the judge, your children, ex-partner/wife/husband, family, friends, colleagues, students, neighbors, parents, and relatives (both dead and alive), the professional community, a religious community, the banker and the accountant, new and imagined associates/colleagues, strangers, the grocer and dry cleaner, the children's teachers, God, to name a few.

What are they saying? What is your response? Does what they are saying influence the opinions you hold of yourself? Do these negative imagined accounts that you perceive others are holding about you influence how you perform your life and how you relate to people?

Counterviewing questions include: Why would this injurious conversation want to separate you from your best knowledge of yourself and the persons that love you? Do you think the divorce has changed every aspect of who you are as a person and has it somehow turned every single person who once loved you against you, including yourself? Do you feel like the problem has supplied you with a negative paparazzi view of yourself? How has the problem created a horrible campaign of gossip about your life? What are your thoughts on gossip and gossipers? Are there any outstanding ideas that you have grown up with concerning marriage that are presently holding you back from a different and perhaps more philosophic/realistic view of your situation? Are there any particular popular knowledges about marriage/divorce that seem to be supporting this negative view of yourself?

These debilitating negative self-surveillance/audience conversations so often disconnect the person from his or her relationships. Implementing a rich process of reconnection toward belonging and re-remembrances regarding the more fulfilling stories that persons in their lives have told about who they are is crucial for change to occur. Watching for and speaking to signs of restored hope and charting hope's comeback (as it tries to push through the habit) is also liberating and helpful.

## Illegitimacy

I was first introduced to the inner workings of this habit in 1997 through the therapeutic work my Vancouver School for Narrative Therapy teaching colleague Vikki Reynolds[17] was doing with Canadian-based refugees who had been victims of torture in their home countries because of their political beliefs. Vikki introduced me to these men, and I worked with them in therapy and experienced a close-up view of their experience of disconnection and illegitimacy. She also introduced me to the political activists' idea of witnessing and legitimizing their experience through a process of therapy (Reynolds, 2010). I then began to extrapolate on these experiences to consider the experience of illegitimacy in the lives of other persons I was talking with in therapy.

This internalized conversational habit involves the question of who has the rights to the person/problem story being told. When problems question a person's legitimacy and human rights, a certain experience of less-than-worthiness takes hold. Persons can come to experience themselves as refugees in their own lives, with nowhere to belong or feel safe. Persons will often recall an experience of feeling fraudulent or deficient in their own lives/relationships. As a side note, many therapists I see in therapy and "super"-vision experience this illegitimate experience.

I question the discourse of illegitimacy in the following counterviewing ways:

- Who holds the power to construct the story of legitimate personhood?
- How are standards of legitimacy produced?
- What place does a feeling of belonging hold in one's experience of legitimacy/illegitimacy?
- By what means are these stories negotiated and circulated?
- What knowledge/power is involved in determining who is normal and who is not normal?
- How do people begin to experience themselves as a refugee in their own life?
- What problem stories and modes of production assist in this story of illegitimacy?
- What alternative stories assist in deconstructing this story of illegitimacy and re-remembering other preferred aspects of ourselves?

---

[17] Vikki Reynolds has been a faculty member with the Vancouver School for Narrative Therapy in Vancouver Canada since 2004. See her work at http://www.therapeuticconversations.com.

Consider the many persons who come to see you in therapy who experience themselves as less-than-worthy citizens, parents, children, therapists, workers, partners, and so on. These are persons who feel they are illegitimate, unworthy, and fraudulent—whether it be the young person who has been violated sexually, or the employee who feels left out, or the gay man who is forced to hide his identity, or the new mother who sees herself as selfish, or the shy person who is afraid to speak, or the overweight individual who cannot go out, or the person on social assistance who is ashamed to be seen by his or her family, or the person of color who quite rightfully feels invisible, or the therapist who feels useless and thinks about quitting his or her job before doing any "more" harm.

The habit of illegitimacy speaks to a person's experience of feeling a lack of connection, visibility, and belonging in his or her everyday life. The injurious speech act of the habit does not make available to that person the many reasons why he or she feels this sense of anomie, through the very fact of living within the dominant norms of Western societies. Instead, the habitual conversation is one of blame and condemns this person for being, as a client once mentioned to me, a "loser in their own life."

If we consider a poststructural position in our questioning, we can begin to hold a person's experience as one connected to a much larger set of punishing values, moral codes, and expectations. Through this discovery, we might begin to piece together a plan to stand up to the oppressive dialogic regimes that hold the person exclusively accountable.

I question the discourse of illegitimacy in the following counterviewing ways:

- Do you have a sense of who is backing up this story that you do not belong?
- Were there ever times that you questioned someone's view of you as illegitimate?
- Are there any views that society holds that make it difficult for you to feel like you are a legitimate citizen?
- Have there been any particular stories told about you by powerful influences (e.g., bosses, books, TV, doctors) that have reinforced your experience of feeling powerless?

- Do you ever find that the more you try and prove your legitimate worth to someone (or some group), the more you end up feeling illegitimate?

## Fear

This discursive habit accesses our greatest fears regarding disconnection, loneliness, and self-doubt. The problem creates a "horror film" of our worst nightmares (past, present, and future), thereby paralyzing our fresh ideas and thwarting any and all attempts to move toward freedom.

I question the discourse of fear in the following counterviewing ways:

- What are the worst fears produced within one's culture (e.g., being poor, being marginalized, being shunned, being single, being left out and not included)?
- What ideas might keep these fears alive within your experience of living?
- How does fear manage to wreak havoc on your imagination?
- By what means does the problem of fear create a frightened state and then blame a person for being a coward?
- How does fear take away from a person's ability to recognize and honor his or her journey?
- In what ways can fear be treated as the scared little problem that it is?
- In what ways can fear be turned on itself and become afraid of a person's moves toward standing up to it?

The habit of an internalized dialogic negative fear is different from legitimate or reasonable fear. Children do need to fear walking into oncoming traffic, sexism/racism/homophobia do exist, dogs do sometimes bite, and planes do sometimes crash. Further, date rape does happen and drinking outdated milk could give you a stomachache. To acknowledge a reasonable fear is very often to construct a plan of safety.

The habit of fear is a different bird altogether. The habitual dialogue that fear promotes is ongoing, insidious, "irrational," and definitely not safe! The conversation creates debilitating scenarios of death, destruction, isolation, and rejection. It has been described as "a pounding physical force that sits atop my chest and squeezes the life out of me." Many dominant narratives play into fear's ability to grow larger in a person's life. Fear acts like the "little engine that could" behind the scenes (like the wizard behind the curtain), conducting a full accounting of all the many ways you will mess up your life—that is, all the ways people will hurt you and reject you and all the many reasons why you should just give up on life.

A tactic of fear (like many of the other habits) is to argue both sides of the "coin" (and damn you no matter what side you take). What I mean by this is that the fear conversation will create a context of frightening scenarios and at the same time blame the person for being fearful (and crazy) for dreaming up these scenarios. This is a second order fear—fear about fear.

Interviewing the injurious speech acts of fear can initially be embarrassing for the person. But it is within this very experience of embarrassment that a person's counterlogic of his or her own abilities to create spaces of safety, acceptance, and strength can be highlighted.

I question the discourse of fear in the following counterviewing ways:

- Do you have a sense that fear has launched a terror campaign against your life?
- Do the fears attempt to box you in and give you no way out, ultimately leading you to a dead end?
- Does this fear ever draw on everyday events around the world and blow them out of proportion by telling you this could happen to you?
- Do you ever catch fear exaggerating?
- Are there ideas common to all of us that fear takes advantage of (e.g., job loss, death, disease, loneliness)?
- Does fear ever make you feel like you are a passenger in your own life?

### Negative Imagination/Invidious Comparison

Negative imagination takes hold across the temporal plain by gathering only negative information from the past and present that fits within the problem frame (Bateson, 1979) and predicts "more of the same" negative results into the future. Negative imagination produces a shallow description of the fullness of lived personhood, leaving out experiences of survival, love, and connection. It produces a constant "worst case scenario" of events. Negative imagination—through invidious comparison—will always compare a person "down." No matter what the circumstance or story, the person is left with the feeling that he or she does not quite "measure up" to specified standards. The tyranny of perfection with its impossible quest often helps this habit along.

I question the discourse of negative imagination and invidious comparison in the following counterviewing ways:

- How does negative imagination capture the complete story of personhood?
- What tactics and allies does it use to create such a convincing story of negativity?
- What common ideas about who you "should be" does it solicit to seal off any alternative lived experience from its account of your life?
- How does negative imagination gather "steam" within the problem story?
- What helps to create a "leak" in the negative imagination framework?
- How is it that persons in our community have been left with the experience that they have not reached nor will they ever reach a culturally acceptable norm?
- Which normalizing views are most effective in maintaining an invidious (unpleasant) negative comparative experience?

One person described negative imagination as a "train without brakes" because once the negatively imagined dialogue gets on a roll, it is very difficult to stop. A mole on your forearm transforms itself into wondering who will attend your funeral, a partner who is late for dinner is imagined in a motel room with the neighbor, a temper tantrum of a young child means the child will never be attending college, and a particular glance from a colleague is interpreted to mean that you will not have your job at the end of the day.

A young woman described invidious comparison as "holding court against her in just about every encounter" she had, from the women on billboards that she saw when walking down the street, to inanimate speakers like animals, to persons she did not know—in her mind, they all compared her down from the person she was "supposed to be." From within the habit's grasp on her life, she believed the model she saw in the magazine was thinking that her body was disgusting, the dog next door never wanted an owner like her, and every stranger she crossed paths with disliked her. To expose and discuss these internalized negative conversations is to poke holes in their legitimacy and what seems to be their ironclad logic.

## Internalized Bickering

Problems' conversations love to debate issues as a tactic of confusion—they don't really care what side of the argument they take, and they will often argue both sides. The bickering is an exhausting process of self-doubt that often leaves a person with no answers and feeling paralyzed. This process is sometimes referred to as the "paralysis of analysis." The internalized argument is often fully capturing of our imagination and creativity.

I question the discourse of internalized bickering in the following counterviewing ways:

- What institutional standards does bickering thrive on?
- What are the agreed on moral codes regarding specified ways of behaving that bickering draws on?
- In what ways does internalized bickering capture the "heart" of our conversations?
- It is said that we speak internally at approximately 1,200 words a minute—how much time does the average person spend on any given day getting caught up in the bickering?
- In what ways can we celebrate and appreciate moments of freedom from this lived experience?
- What would it mean to be free of problem-centered bickering?

Think about the prospect of quitting your job, or reliving a difficult conversation with a loved one, or trying to decide whether to quit smoking. The habit of internalized bickering can completely capture a person's entire conversational domain (with just one of these topics, never mind the hundreds of decisions we make on a daily basis).

The habit's injurious speech acts to argue, counterargue, and argue some more from differing positions (and other persons' positions) over and over again across the temporal plain. Members of the Vancouver Anti-Anorexia/Bulimia League commented on their experience with internalized bickering, stating how it was such "exhausting work" trying to keep up with the "right" thing to do. And even after a decision was made, a conversation could be had on whether it was the right decision! Round and round and round they went. Add to this the other habits—particularly the habit of the self-surveillance/audience—and you can see how a person can be trapped inside a hundred different positions the imagined others would take and not take, support and not support, on any given issue. Talk like this can take up so much of our lived experience that we end up experiencing very little else but indecisions.

In the horrid and often murderous conversational domain of disordered eating, internalized bickering takes on enormous proportions (see Grieves, 1998; Madigan & Epston, 1995). Internal debate regarding calorie counting, number crunching, exercising, body surveillance, whether to do 1,000 or 1,500 sit-ups, and the shoulds and should nots about practically every subject are in constant discussion. The end result is that a person's close-up attention to all the habits' issues is distracting them from moving forward (as they are eternally calculated as either entirely wrong or not quite perfect enough). David Epston has likened this phenomenon to being "crucified to a dilemma" (D. Epston, personal communication, July, 2002).

The process of internalized bickering erodes confidence, support, and trust in one's self. A person once came to see me because the person's family members could not decide whether their terminally sick, nonspeaking Mother should be cremated or buried in a casket. The family members bickering had completely taken over their lives, and the all-consuming effects of this ongoing debate had forced them to lose their relationships with each other (during a time of immanent loss). This resulted in family members becoming very isolated and disconnected from one another.

A heterosexual couple came to see me regarding their ongoing relationship conflicts. We discovered that the number of times they bickered "out loud" with each other was a startling "100 times less" than the number of discussions they had internally (about the issues), meaning that they came to realize that the main conflict between them was being viciously played out within their individual personal discussions regarding whether to stay or to go that they were having within themselves. They also discovered that they sometimes had a difficult time figuring out what they had actually said and done between them compared with what they had imagined. Once they found mutual ways to stop their internalized bickering within themselves (thereby stopping the imagined internalized bickering with the other), the actual issues of conflict between them were easily sorted through and eventually resolved.

Another person came to see me and said that despite the fact she had tested negative three times, she remained convinced she was infected by the HIV virus. Once again, the internalized bickering and its punishing effects had taken over her life, and she had begun to give up and lose everything she once loved.

Not all internalized bickering has the dramatic and negative consequences of the prior examples; however, the habit does provide a foundation for temporary paralysis, bitterness, mistrust, compelling thoughts, thoughtlessness, and as one client stated, "a devotion to time not very well spent." I would liken the habit to the mindless torture Sisyphus endured as he pushed that boulder up the hill only to watch it roll down the other side when he reached the top.

More counterviewing questions are: Do you have a take on who's arguing for and who is arguing against these many internal bickerings? Are there ever times that you can look back and address how much of your day was spent bickering with yourself? Have there been times when you have become fed up and exhausted with these "ongoing nowhere" conversations? Do you ever stop to notice the calm you experience when the internal bickering quiets down? Have you ever experienced yourself listening in on the bickering and finding it amusing? Have you ever been aware of what and who might sit behind this dialogue outside of yourself?

## Hopelessness

This injurious conversational habit affords a cascading downward view that renders all help, community, and connection pointless. It is a surrender to the belief that all hopeful experience and stories that live outside the problem frame are meaningless. It is a tactical strategy that affords the problem possibility for "giving up" on all things possible.

I question the discourse of hopelessness in the following counterviewing ways:

- What are the combined problem efforts that afford an experience of hopelessness?
- How does your community view a person's sense of hopelessness?
- What institutional discourse and practices support hopelessness?
- What are the alternative practices that support hope?
- What specific issue does hopelessness thrive on?
- Is there any particular belief or anyone person that most assists a hopeless view of yourself?
- Was there ever a time that you experienced a little bit of hope for yourself?

Hopelessness takes many forms, and most steer us toward an experience of us giving up on ourselves (Anderson, 1987). Persons describe the feeling as an experience of "no way out," "being boxed in," and "life being futile." Hopelessness inspires a sad paralysis of belief and performance. Hopelessness directs persons toward a dead-end view of their lives. It encapsulates our lived experience into a small and limiting picture.

Remember Tom's experience of going free of depression? On retirement from a long and successful career (as reported by his partner), Tom came to see me with very "little desire for living left." Hopelessness offered him an extremely shallow retrospective view of the life he had lived and predicted that it "would only get worse." He had been pushed along in hopelessness, with the help of an 11-month stay on the psychiatric ward, to the point at which he decided that a choice of killing himself was a better one than a choice of life.

A 35-year-old woman who described her life as mired in isolation and hopelessness came to see me. During our 3 months of therapy together, she began to take steps toward a renewed hope in herself by taking university courses, reconnecting with friends, enrolling in recreational activities, and visiting with family. To celebrate her newfound hope, she invited a friend to go on a 1-week kayaking trip as a way to celebrate her re-membering back to all the qualities and gifts hopelessness had once taken from her. She had just returned from the trip when she came to see me again. She described being in an "awful state" because on her return to home, hopelessness took a gigantic and vicious step back into her life—so much so that she had made a serious attempt to take her life. Fortunately, the emergency service team got to her "in the nick of time" to save her. We realized together that we had mistakenly underplayed the necessity to plan for a return of hopelessness on her return from her trip. The anger she felt toward herself was suddenly turned against the hopelessness habit for attempting to "wash away my memories of my trip and the strides forward I made these past few months." She stated that "swallowing the pills was not me and never again will the fake and made-up story of hopelessness take over my life!" She is now able to maintain the hope in her life that she worked so hard to bring back and has not chosen a step toward death in several months.

A young person 15 years of age quietly relayed a sad story of being bullied and rejected throughout the course of his school and neighborhood life. A daily conversation of hopelessness had entered his life and given him very little to aspire to. Hopelessness encouraged a view that his existence "would only get worse." Hopelessness had blocked any other view of himself such as excellent student, community volunteer, humorous person, solid skateboarder, and good at helping friends get through "rough times" that he was eventually able to recall.

I question the discourse of hopelessness in the following counterviewing ways:

- Do you thinking that giving up on hope is the way in which hopelessness finds a way to help you believe that giving up is a good answer?
- Are there places of hope that you can remember that are currently blocked out by hopelessness?
- Is there any one person or any one idea that promotes hopelessness within your day-to-day living?
- If hope were to be rediscovered in your life, what present qualities in you would give it staying power?

- Is the love you hold for yourself in any way helpful to the restoration of hope in your life?

## Perfection

Perfection masks itself in the world of acceptable forms of high achievement and attitudes of excellence. Although there is obvious room to appreciate one's evolving achievements and to try one's best in any endeavor to work hard, to learn more, and to excel at one's passion, negative discourse and the possibility of injurious perfection speech is ever present given the discursive pressure toward perfection ideals within Western cultures.

We are trained in ideas of perfection through most of our learning lives within the teachings and structures of religion, education, athletics, science, media, medicine, industry, and so on. Perfection standards (despite being entirely unachievable and mythical) are underwritten by humanist ideas of the "higher self." This particular habit plays a dominant role in our experience of not measuring up to specified standards of living. Although perfection is not humanly possible, the discourses in which perfection is located continue to hound us with the idea that we should continue to pursue it with ever greater zeal. Perfection training often dismisses our achievements and categorizes them as "not quite good enough." We might have cause to wonder if we are inspired to train harder for ourselves or for perfection.

I question the discourse of negative imagination and invidious comparison in the following counterviewing ways:

- Can you recall the ways in which you have been trained and pressured into ideas of perfection even though perfection is not possible?
- In what ways do perfection standards make you blind to your achievements as a person, parent, partner, employee, and so forth?
- If you were to reject your training in perfection ideals, what aspects of yourself and the efforts you have made should be celebrated?
- Has the idea of perfection in any way given you a less-than-worthy idea of yourself?
- In what ways does perfection negate your ability to listen to another's praise of you?

- Does perfection seem to measure the cup of achievement as being half empty?
- Do you have a sense that you could ever satisfy the critical voice of perfection?
- Are the pressures of perfection any different between men and women?

I have always intended to write a book entitled *I'm Not OK, You're Not OK—and That's OK!* as a way of undermining the curse of the idea of perfection. Through my work alongside my longtime colleague Lorraine Grieves (see Grieves, 1998) and the years of co-research conducted with the Vancouver Anti-Anorexia/Bulimia League, it became clear that the struggle to undermine the pressures of perfection that the membership experienced was paramount. We came to realize that the habit of perfection would never allow a person to experience a joy for living. Perfection, as one member stated, "set such high standards, and once I got there it always moved the bar a little higher." For example, perfection helped set the preferred weight a woman should lose and, once that weight was attained, there was no room for celebration because perfection would move the perfect weight "just a little lower." Perfection discourse demanded just a little more exercise, just a little less food, just a few more laxatives, and so on. This vicious game of perfection would often continue until the person could no longer function and ended up hospitalized. And, sadly, there were times when the perfection game ended in death.

Perfection was once described to me as an "angry taskmaster" and one that is "punishing, blaming, and persecuting." The tortured struggle to achieve perfection as a student, dancer, daughter, worker, parent, athlete, boss, partner, etc., can ruin lives. Perfection discourse appears to have no boundaries as to whom it negatively affects.

A high-ranking business executive recently came to see me through an executive health network. He worked an average of 14 hours a day on his climb up the corporate ranks. He rarely took more than a day or two off a month for fear of "falling behind." When he wasn't working, he was at the gym trying to sculpt the perfect corporate body.[18] He stated that he

---

[18] David Epston has called this experience one of "corporate anorexia."

often felt that despite all of his hard work, he could not keep up with the pressures and manage the stress of the corporate agenda that supported perfection. He stated that he was "miserable and never had time to dwell on his achievements." He was only 38 years old when years of injurious perfection harassment had helped bring on the heart attack that almost killed him.[19] In the aftermath of his 8-day hospital stay, he let me know that perfection told him he was "weak and feeling sorry for himself" and needed to "keep working as hard as he had before." He feared the heart attack "would lesson his value in the eyes of his peers." Perfection had set up his dangerous health conditions and then blamed him for his current position of ill health. Perfection then demanded that he "get back up on the horse again and stop worrying—worry was for losers."

Even when people experience being sacrificed on the altar of perfection, they can sometimes find it very difficult to take a step back and look at the life that perfection had driven them toward. It could be argued that perfection—working in tandem with all the other injurious conversational habits—provides the fuel for that hard-driving machine known as corporate America.

## Guilt

A constant training in this conversational habit comes by way of our trainings in such institutional discourses as religion, science, corporate and academic institutions, and so forth, coupled with dominant and specified ways of performing in gender, class, sexual preference, race, and so on. When guilt leaks its way into our imagination and understandings, it can flow without restraint. Guilt will often set the stage for a wealth of other problem strategies and misunderstandings to emerge.

I question the discourse of guilt in the following counterviewing ways:

- When you look at history, what conversations of guilt have been used as instruments of social control?

---

[19] Cocaine use is usually a primary cause of heart attacks with other clients I see under the age of 40. This was not the case for this client.

- By what historical means has the conversation of guilt been used to sway the populous into specific ways of being?
- Who are usually positioned to be the beneficiaries of guilt?
- What are the combined effects of guilt on communities, families, and persons?
- Have there ever been times that guilt has persuaded you into doing things or saying things that left you feeling empty afterwards?
- Are there experiences in your life that you have been wrongly guilted for?
- Have you ever in your heart done what you considered to be the right thing but somehow guilt blamed you for doing the wrong thing? How do you explain this?
- Do you think men and women are equally trained up in guilt?

A lawyer came to see me last week for "a talk." His law partners asked him to come and see me because they viewed him as "not being a team player." The issue at hand was that he had refused to give the firm his telephone number while he was away on a 1-week vacation. Although he fully justified his position to me, he also stated that he still "felt a bit guilty for not giving his number out" because this was a common practice of all the lawyers in his firm.

A young man recently came to see me to discuss a guilt he experienced after coming forward to the authorities about being sexually abused by a clergy member during his childhood. The clergy member in question was now being investigated (there had been a number of other complaints). The young man began to have "second thoughts" about his courage to come forward after many persons of the congregation, a family member, and an old friend had disagreed with his decision. He discussed that he felt himself "between a rock and a hard place" because he experienced guilt during the time he was silent about the abuse and guilt after he had divulged the information. Conversations of guilt argued both sides.

A woman came to see me to discuss her wanting to leave her abusive husband. The woman was the mother of three teenage daughters ages 13, 15, and 18 years. She stated that her husband's ongoing verbal and occasional physical abuse had begun during her first pregnancy. She had pondered the possibility of leaving him for many years but had stayed with him because she felt guilty "on account of the children." She also described her experience of guilt for not leaving him, believing herself to be "too weak to leave" and feeling that she was a "horrible role model for her daughters." Guilt spoke to both sides of the leaving/staying equation and was supported by many ideological (and competing) discursive factions.

## NAMING AND WRITING PRACTICES

Narrative therapy views the idea of change, what constitutes change, and what is considered change under the direct influence of a therapy's conversational boundaries, linguistic territories, cultural structures, and performance of theory (Madigan, 2007). Therapeutic understanding, response, and action is shaped by and shaping of these discursive parameters, offering discursive "life" to both hopeful and despairing ideas (sometimes simultaneously) concerning the possibility of change.

Narrative therapy attempts to render transparent the process of cultural production and reproduction in therapy, while also offering a possible alternative to current institutionalized naming and writing therapy practices. Narrative practices address the influence these processes have on the construction of hope and change. There are numerous narrative methods to address the possibility of hope and change through a variety of writing and naming practices.[20]

The psychological practice of classifying persons and writing their histories into historical documents (files), through the template of "soft" scientific research and investigation, has, for narrative therapists, acted to re-produce set cultural and institutional norms (Foucault, 1973; Parker, 1998; Reynolds, 2008, 2010; Said, 2003; Spivak 1996). What is re-produced within the name given to a person is not only a newly inscribed identity politic but also a verification (perhaps a valorization) that uplifts the legitimacy of scientific research and the status of the profession itself.

Within a name (e.g., obsessive–compulsive disorder, borderline personality disorder), one's body is naturally inscribed by science and the

---

[20] My particular version of narrative therapy includes the use of Foucault's and poststructural ideas, counterviewing questions, therapeutic letter-writing campaigns, and the creation of communities of concern.

privileged status given to the naming and writing context (Grieves, 1998; Sanders, 2007). Unfortunately, the everyday act of professional naming and writing the bodies of persons (and groups of persons) into categories is often a finalized, decontextualized, and pathologizing view of who the persons are and who they might become (Caplan & Cosgrove, 2004; S. Spear, personal communication, 2009). The client is often instructed to anticipate the limits of his or her life course in particular and nonhopeful ways (Caplan, 1995; Sanders, 1998).

Deciphering the person/problem named is usually a matter of interpreting and categorizing a "cause" to explain the presenting problem (Dickerson & Zimmerman, 1996). The cause (more often than not) is located and privatized within the person's abnormal body and genetically linked to other members of their family unit and their abnormal bodies. Within this model of scientific naming and writing, the body of the subject/client (you and me) is viewed as the passive tablet on which disordered names are written.

Entering a helping system like a psychiatric hospital, a child-care center, or a therapy clinic, the client is often required, because of insurance company claims and third-party billing, to accept a disordered name before therapy can proceed. The name is further secured by the naming performance when it is entered into professional filing sites (Foucault, 1979)—for example, insurance, education, medical, judicial, or corporate files. The history of our life file is cumulative and can sometimes last forever.

Professional stories written and told about the person—to the person prescribed and to others—can maintain the powerfully pathologized plot, rhetorically embed the problem name (and personal life), and assist in piecing together states of despair. For people looking for help and change, the naming and writing process of therapy used in North America can be both confusing and traumatic (Epston, 2009; Jenkins, 2009; Madigan, 2007). Their answer to hope and possibility is to undergo further practices of therapeutic technology/pharmacology deemed hopeful and in concert with the practices of help offered to them by the very institution that named them. If they fail to change within the therapeutic parameters prescribed, the body will be further named (Moules, 2003).

The consequence of an ideologically biased commerce of problems regularly finds a person's constructed identity very misrepresented and underknown by dominant knowledge and sets of agreed-on "thin conclusions" (M. White, personal communication, 1990). Both the process of spoken and written pathologizing and the technologies imported to implement the discourse of pathology speak volumes about the dominant signifying mental health culture but little of the person being described.

## NEW FORMS OF WRITING AND NAMING: THERAPEUTIC LETTER-WRITING CAMPAIGNS

Therapeutic letter-writing campaigns[21] (Madigan, 2004, 2008; Madigan & Epston, 1995) assist people to re-remember lost aspects of themselves. The campaigns assist persons to be re-membered (I. McCarthy, personal communication, 1998; Myerhoff, 1992; M. White, personal communication, 1994) back toward membership systems of love and support from which the problem has dis-membered them.

The logic behind the community letter-writing campaign is one response to the problem identity growing stronger within the structures of the institution (see Gremillion, 2003; Madigan & Goldner, 1998) and within the many other systems that seem to help problems along. There is a correlation between the person being cut off from hope and forgotten experiences of themselves and relationships that lived outside of their "sick" identity and the rapidly growing professional file of hopelessness.

Creating letter-writing campaigns through communities of concern was a therapeutic means to counterbalance the issue of the problem-saturated story and memory (Madigan, 1997). Campaigns recruited a community of re-membering and loving others who held on to preferred stories of the client while the client was restrained by the problem. Their lettered stories lived outside the professional and cultural inscription that defined the person suffering and were also stories that stood on the belief that change was possible.

---

[21] I created therapeutic letter-writing campaigns as an extension of Epston and White's numerous practices of the written word.

Letter-writing campaigns have been designed for persons as young as 6 years and as old as 76 years. Community-based campaigns have assisted persons struggling with a wide assortment of difficulties, including anxiety, child loss, HIV/AIDS, bulimia, depression, perfection, fear, and couple conflict. The campaigns create a context in which it becomes possible for people struggling with problems to bring themselves back from the depths of the problem's grip, formidable isolation, self-harm, and attempts that choose death over life (Madigan & Epston, 1995).

Persons receiving letters begin to rediscover a discourse of the self that assists them to re-member back into situations from which the problem has most often dis-membered them (Hedtke & Winslade, 2004/2005; Sanders, 1997; Sanders & Thompson, 1994). These include claiming back former membership associations with intimate relationships, school, sports, careers, and family members and becoming reacquainted with aspects of themselves once restrained by the problem identity.

Over the years, we have encouraged massive international writing campaigns that net literally hundreds of responses and have had equally successful three-person problem blockades. Throughout this time, letters of support have arrived from some very curious authors. For example, letters of support and hope have been "written" by family dogs, teddy bears, cars, dead grandparents, unborn siblings, and unknown movie stars (see campaign contributors later in this chapter).

## TRAVELS WITH OSCAR

A colleague referred 70-year-old Oscar and his wife, Maxine, to me. In our first session, Oscar informed me that he had been struck down by a truck at a crosswalk a year before. He was not supposed to have lived, but he did; he was not supposed to have come out of his 3-month-long coma, but he did; and it was predicted that he would never walk again, but he did; and so on. As you might imagine, it didn't take me long to realize that I was sitting before a remarkable man. However, it seemed that Oscar had paid dearly for his comeback because somewhere along the way he had lost all "confidence" in himself. He also told me he would panic if Maxine was not by his side "24 hours a day."

Maxine had spent the year before organizing the complicated task of Oscar's medical care and was, at the time of our first visit, looking forward to getting back to her own business pursuits. Unfortunately, her interests were being pushed aside and taken over by what they both called *anxiety.*

The conversational experience of anxiety that had been the "legacy" of Oscar's accident had him believing that "I am only half a man," and furthermore, "Maxine will leave me for another man," and "I believe she is planning to put me in an old-age home." Anxiety also had him believing that "I did not deserve a good life" and, furthermore, "I should kill myself." The relationship with anxiety was allowing him to remember to forget the life he had lived prior to the accident. Oscar also let me know that he was becoming more and more "isolated and depressed."

Oscar and Maxine told me that they had moved from England to Canada 10 years earlier and that their life together had been "blissful" before the accident. In the first session, we all agreed that the anxiety was gaining on Oscar and that the situation was, as Oscar stated, "desperate." During the next session, we decided to design an international anti-anxiety letter-writing campaign. Exhibit 4.4 shows the letter we coauthored in 5 minutes near the end of the second session (it can be viewed as a standard letter-writing campaign letter). As Oscar was concerned that his friends might consider the letter "a crazy idea," he insisted that I include my credentials to give it "credence" (Oscar's words from our sessions are in quotation marks).

The structure of campaign letters is usually the same. Together with the client, I write a letter to members of the family/community (whom the client and/or family member selects) and ask them to assist in a temporal re-remembering and witnessing process through lettered written accounts outlining (a) their memories of their relationship with the client, (b) their current hopes for the client, and (c) how they anticipated their relationship growing with the client in the future.

These written accounts are directed squarely at countering the problems' strategies to re-write a person's past as only negative and project a future filled only with the hopelessness of worst-case scenarios. The letters also begin to re-write any negative professionalized stories found to be unhelpful to the person and helpful to the problem. And, the letters

**Exhibit 4.4    Letter Sent to Oscar's Friends**

Dear Friends of Oscar:

My name is Stephen Madigan and I have an MSW as well as an MSc and PhD in family therapy. Your friends Oscar and Maxine have asked me to write to you so that we might solicit your support. As you are probably aware, Oscar suffered a terrible accident 14 months ago, and he has instituted a remarkable comeback. What you may not know is that the aftereffects of the accident have left Oscar a captive of anxiety, and anxiety is currently bossing him around. You may not believe this, but one of the messages anxiety gives to Oscar is that "he is a good-for-nothing," that "he is a useless human being," and that "sooner than later all of his friends will come to know him the way anxiety knows him."

Through anxiety's influence, Oscar is beginning to "give up on himself," and we ask your support in bringing him back from anxiety's grip. We all agree that as his chosen community of concern, you can help Oscar win back his life from this terrible anxiety.

Could you please send Oscar a brief letter expressing (a) how you remember your history with him, (b) your thoughts and feelings about his physical comeback and his person in the present, and (c) how you believe you would like to see your relationship with Oscar (and Maxine) be in the future.

We hope that your letters of support are not too much to ask, and we want you to know that they will be greatly appreciated. Oscar would like all of you to know that he will respond to all of your replies.

Warm regards,

Stephen Madigan, PhD, Oscar's Anti-Anxiety Consultant

sent to the person are always diametrically different from what had been written previously in the client's file. Campaign letters written by the person's community of concern re-present a counterfile. Documenting alternative versions counteract the infirming effects of the professional and cultural problem story and the pathologized names inscribed onto the person's body.

During the weeks that followed, Oscar would bring the campaign letters to my office and request that I read them out loud to him (his eyesight was poor on account of the accident). I happily did so, and my recitations were accompanied by Oscar's crying, laughing, and telling me "of his good fortune."[22] The letters helped him begin to remember more alternative stories; he also made the decision to "get off" the medication his psychiatrist had prescribed him over a year before. We also invited a few of his friends and family to come to the sessions to read out loud the letters they had written to Oscar (see the discussion of campaign therapy session structure below).

As the content of the letters documented, Oscar had affected many, many lives. Not surprisingly, his community of concern welcomed the opportunity to reciprocate by writing to him with their support and love. His anti-anxiety support team wrote from places around the globe, including Europe, the United Kingdom, and North America.

A few months later, Oscar wrote to me from his long-awaited "anti-anxiety" trip to France with Maxine. He once stated that the trip to France would mark "my arrival back to health." He wrote on the postcard that he was sitting alone, drinking espresso, while Maxine had gone sight seeing for the day. He wrote, "I am thanking my lucky stars that I am no longer a prisoner of anxiety." His said that the only problem now was "keeping up with all of his return correspondence!" But he stated that the return correspondence was a problem he could manage and was willing to take "full responsibility for."

Without the recruitment of a community of concern, Oscar might never have rebounded to re-remember all his personal abilities/qualities

---

[22] It is now the everyday practice of letter-writing campaigns to bring the writers into the session to read their letters to the person as an act of re-telling.

and the contributions he had made during his lifetime that the problem was "insisting" be overlooked and he be dis-remembered from.

Letter-writing campaigns are viewed as attempts to counter the problem's cultural and professional disinformation. They also inform the client, family, and community about those "stories" of the person that are at odds with the problem-saturated story. Campaigns are viewed not only as ceremonies of re-definition (White, 1995b) but also as protest and counterstruggles to undermine a problem-contextualized dominant story.

The logic behind the community letter-writing campaign is also an attempt at finding ways to respond to certain problem identities growing stronger within the structures of the institution. Often a tension exists between persons in the hospital/institution/child-care facility (because of their being cut off from hope and forgotten experiences of themselves) and the relational identities that live outside of their "sick" identity. This is a tension worthy of exploration. My practiced of narrative therapy in part hinges on creating counterbalances within the tension by including a community of re-membering and loving others who hold the stories of the client while the client is temporarily too restrained by the problem to remember these preferred and alternative memories. These desired stories live outside the professional and cultural inscription that defines the person suffering and stand on the belief that change is always possible (Smith & Nylund, 1997).

## LETTER-WRITING CAMPAIGN STRUCTURE

Letter-writing efforts can take on a variety of shapes and forms, but the most standard campaigns involve the following (Madigan, 1999, 2004, 2008):

1.  The campaign emerges from a narrative interview when alternative accounts of who the person might be are questioned, revived, and re-remembered. Persons are asked to consider whether there are other people who may regard them differently from how the problem describes them. These different accounts are then spoken of. I might ask the following questions: "If I were to interview _____ about you, what do you think they might tell me about yourself that the problem would not dare to tell me?" Or "Do you think your friend's

telling of you to me about you would be an accurate telling, even if it contradicted the problem's tellings of you?" Or "Whose description of you do you prefer, and why?"

2. Together, the client and I (along with the client's family/partner, friend, therapist, insiders, and so on, if any of these persons are in attendance) begin a conversation regarding all the possible other descriptions of the client as a person that the client might have forgotten to remember because of the problem's hold over him or her. We dialogue on who the client might be, who the client would like to be, and who the client used to be well before the problem took over his or her life. We recall the forgotten alternative lived experiences of himself or herself that the client may have forgotten through the problem's restraining context.

3. We then begin to make a list of all the persons in the client's life who would be in support of these alternative descriptions. Once the list is complete, we construct a letter of support and invitation.

4. If finances are a problem, my Yaletown Family Therapy office supplies the envelopes and stamps for the ensuing campaign.

5. If privacy is an issue, we use Yaletown Family Therapy as the return address.

6. The preference is for as many of the letter writers from the community of concern to attend the sessions as possible. If the person comes to the next session (with the letters) alone, I will offer to read the letters back to the person as a textual re-telling.

7. The client is asked to go through the collection of letters as a way of conducting a "re-search" on himself or herself.

The general structure for reading and witnessing the letters in therapy is as follows:

1. All campaign writers are invited to the session (if this is geographically possible) and in turn are asked to read aloud the letter they have penned about the person. In attendance is usually the client, myself, the other writers from their community, and sometimes a therapy team that may include insiders.

2.  After each writer reads aloud, the client is asked to read the letter back to the writer, so both writer and client can attend to what is being said/written from the different positions of speaking and listening.
3.  After each letter is read by the writer and discussed with the client, the community of others in the session (who are sitting and listening) offer a brief reflection of what the letter evoked in their own personal lives.
4.  This process continues until all letters are read, reread, responded to, and reflected on.[23]
5.  Reflecting team members[24] (usually but not always professionals;[25] T. Andersen, 1987) then write and read a short letter to the client and his or her community. They reflect on the counterview of the client offered up by the person and his or her community, the hope that was shared, and aspects of the letters that moved them personally.
6.  Copies are made of each letter and given to everyone in attendance.
7.  I then follow up the session with a therapeutic letter addressed to everyone who attended the session including the client, the community of concern, and the reflecting team.

## LETTER CAMPAIGN CONTRIBUTORS

The repercussions of many problems can often push persons to dis-member themselves from the support systems that surround them and coerce them toward isolation, detachment, and withdrawal. Similarly, problems and professional systems may compel support persons to move away from the persons struggling by encouraging hopelessness, anger, and despair.

Our experience has shown that once support persons have received a letter inviting them to contribute to a campaign, they will often feel compelled to write more than once (three and four letters are not uncommon). Contributors often state that they have had the experience of feeling "left

---

[23] See Michael White's (1995b) work on definitional ceremony.

[24] After playing at the World Ultimate Frisbee tournament with Canada in Oslo in 1990, Norwegian psychiatrist Tom Andersen was gracious enough to take me along on a 4-day holiday with him and his family to his summer home in Christensen, Norway. I interviewed him day and night about his new reflecting team practice and his ideas on the art and importance of listening in therapy.

[25] In some campaigns, I have asked former client insiders or members of the Anti-Anorexia/Bulimia League to sit in on the session as insiders.

out" of the helping process. Contributors to the campaign have reported feeling "blamed" and "guilty" for the role they believe they have played in the problem's dominance over the person's life. They suggest that many of these awkward feelings about themselves have been helped along by various professional discourses and self-help literature. Being left out can often leave them with the opinion that they are "impotent" and "useless" (Madigan, 2004).

Letter campaign authors explain that their contributions have helped them feel "useful" and "part of a team." In addition, the writing of a re-remembering text offers family members and other support persons an opportunity to break free of the problem's negative dominance in their own lives and allows for an alternative and active means for renewal and hope. As one older man who committed himself to an antidepression campaign for his 22-year-old nephew explained, "The letter campaign helped me to come off the bench and score big points against the problem so my nephew could pull off a win. In helping him I helped myself."

Therapeutic letter-writing campaigns act to re-remember alternative accounts of a person's lived experience that a problem often separates him or her from. The campaign encourages the person to become reacquainted with the membership groups that the problem has separated him or her from (e.g., family, friends, school, sports, teams, music, painting). Therapeutic letter-writing campaigns are designed as counterpractices to the dis-membering effects of problem lifestyles and the isolating effects that psychological discourses often create in persons' lives. The letters form a dialogic context of preferred re-membering, re-remembering, and meaning. The following is an account of one such campaign.

## TRAVELS WITH PETER

The social work department of an in-patient, adult psychiatric ward asked if I would see Peter, a 38-year-old White, heterosexual, married, middle-class man who worked in the local film industry. This particular psychiatric ward had referred individuals and families to me in the past. The referring social worker also knew that I was the primary therapist responsible for the film and television industry personnel in Vancouver. So it seemed from the social worker's point of view that Peter and I were potentially a good therapeutic match.

Peter was described to me by hospital professionals as "chronically depressed" and was given very little hope for change. The pessimism was triggered as a result of his recent attempts to kill himself while on the ward and having to be physically restrained for pushing a male orderly. The hospital's plan for health and change involved group and individual cognitive–behavioral therapy together with numerous medications. Despite these attempts, hospital staff described to me that "nothing seemed to be working." I was also informed that the staff was beginning to think that after 6 months of ward time, "change was impossible."

Peter had a total of nine visits with me over the course of 4 months. After the first six meetings, he was able to return home from the hospital. All therapy sessions included a narrative reflecting team (Madigan 1991a). On five of the visits, volunteers in the letter-writing campaign (including family members; longtime friends; and his former partner, Caitland, whom he had separated himself from) were invited into therapy to perform their written work "live" in front of Peter.

During the first interview, Peter explained that 11 months prior to our talk, his 3-year-old daughter (whose mother was his former partner, Caitland) had died in a tragic drowning accident. He stated that initially he had only felt "bitter and angry" and "cut off" from the "real meaning to life" and he had "turned down support from anyone that mattered."

Peter stated that he responded to his daughter's death by "barricading myself away from the world" and that "I blamed myself." Shortly thereafter, he separated from his marriage "to be alone." In a short period of time, Peter had virtually removed himself from anyone who cared about him. He was eventually admitted to the ward after a neighbor found him "in the garage with the motor running."

The problem, which he referred to as "an inability to go on," had taken over his daily life. He let us know that he was "haunted day and night" and "couldn't remember much of his life" from before the day his daughter Mara died. He said that he "felt hopeless" and could not remember the "sound of Mara's voice."

Briefly, I outline below a few therapeutic counterviewing questions that Peter and I engaged in:

- Do you think that "giving up on hope" is the way in which your conversations with hopelessness find a way to help you believe that giving up is a good answer—the only answer?
- How do you think the community looks on a father who has lost his 3-year-old daughter?
- Do you feel it is fair that everyone keeps telling you that you'll "get over it"?
- Do you believe that these people believe that there is a proper time line for a grieving father?
- Are there places of past hope that you can remember that are currently blocked out by hopelessness and despair?
- How is this hope possible?
- Do you find any hope in the fact that Dave, your neighbor, pulled you out of the garage before death took you?
- Do you feel that it is a fair accusation to blame yourself for Mara's death? What supports this accusation?
- Was the hospital accurate in diagnosing you as depressed or do you think it might be about your experience of not knowing "how to go on"?
- Why do you think the hospital gave a grieving father so much medication?
- Are there people in your life and community, including the hospital staff, who you believe blame you for Mara's death?
- Has this deep sorrow you've explained to me been a sorrow that you could share with anyone else?
- Is there any one person or any one idea that promotes a life of hopelessness within your day-to-day living?
- Is there anyone in your life, looking in on your life, who you think holds out hope for you—by holding your hope for you—until you return to it?
- If for a moment you could imagine that hope could be re-discovered in your life, what present qualities in you would give it staying power?
- Was there ever a time that you disputed your internal conversations of blame and hopelessness?

- Is the love you hold for Mara in any way helpful to the restoration of hope in your life?

After three sessions, Peter, the team, and I drafted a letter to his community of concern (see Exhibit 4.5). He chose a dozen people to mail the letter to.

---

### Exhibit 4.5    Letter Sent to Peter's Friends and Family

Dear Friends and Family of Peter,

My name is Stephen Madigan, and I am a family therapist working alongside Peter. Since Mara's tragic death, Peter has let me know that "he hasn't known how to face the world." Until recently, a sense of "hopelessness" pretty much "took over his life" to the point that it almost killed him. Another debilitating aspect of this profound loss is that Peter can't "remember much of his life" since before Mara's death. Peter also feels in an "odd way responsible for Mara's death," even though he knows "somewhere in his mind" that he "was out of town the day of the accident." Peter believes that there is a "strong message out there" that he "should just get on with his life." Peter says he finds this attitude "troubling" because each "person is different" and he believes that he "might never get over it but eventually learn to live alongside it."

We are writing to ask you to write a letter in support of Peter explaining (a) memories of your life with Peter, (b) what you shared, (c) who Mara was to you, (d) how you plan to support Peter while he grieves, (e) what Peter has given to you in your life, and (f) what you think your lives will be like together once he leaves the hospital.

Thank you for your help,

Peter, Stephen, and the Team

---

Personally, I found the reflections and readings with Peter and the eight members of his community of concern who attended to be extremely profound. Our letter-writing campaign meetings sometimes lasted 2 to 3 hours (we scheduled them at day's end). Suffice it to say that the texts written by the community of concern acted on Peter's anticipation of hope, acceptance of who he was, and his willingness to further live his life.

Four weeks later, Peter left the hospital on a forward-stepping path to be free of medication and concern. He and Mara's mother, Caitland, then entered into therapy with me to try and restore their marriage. They brought the letters. Together they anticipated the possibility that they could reconstruct their marriage. Hope is a wonderful potion.

There are many other wonderful narrative therapy practices that continue to come forward, and many others that I wish I could have unpacked and attended to more in this chapter. However, space restraints would not allow this.

## INSIDER LEAGUES AND CO-RESEARCH

During the early 1980s, David Epston and Michael White invented an approach to therapy that involved therapeutic letter writing.[26, 27] At least half of their *Narrative Means to Therapeutic Ends* text explains their work through the use of therapeutic letters. Therapeutic letters are viewed as counterdocuments to those files being compiled throughout other systems. White and Epston (1990) wrote that "the proliferation and elevated status of the modern document are reflected by the fact that it is increasingly relied upon for a variety of decisions about the worth of progress" and in the domain the professional disciplines, a document can serve several purposes, "not the least of which is the presentation of the 'self' of the subject of the document and of its author" (p. 188).

Much of the information on the history of documents and the file was garnered from the works of Michel Foucault and psychologist Rom

---

[26] Letter writing was such an integral part of their therapy practice that their initial title for their seminal book *Narrative Means to Therapeutic Ends* was *Literate Means to Therapeutic Ends.*

[27] For a full reading of therapeutic letter writing, see White and Epston (1990) and Dulwich Centre Publications.

Harre (Davies & Harre, 1990). In contemplating psychiatry, Harre put his efforts toward uncovering the "file speak" within a client document (file) and how, over time, the file began to take on a life of its own. He wrote that "a file has an existence and a trajectory through the social world, which soon takes it outside the reach of its subject" (Davies & Harre, 1990, p. 159).

Epston and White regularly sent letters to clients after their session. They wrote to secure subordinate stories, recap appreciation and survival, and ask more questions about the knowledges and alternative stories the client gained through the re-authoring session.[28]

David Epston took the practice of letter writing further and began to circulate his letters and the client's return letters to other clients who remained trapped within the confines of particular problem lifestyles (Epston & White, 1990). He collected their client wisdom in what he called an *archive*. The archive contained an assortment of audiotapes, letter writings, and artwork that represented a rich supply of solutions to an assortment of long-standing problems such as temper taming, night fears, school refusing, bedwetting, bullying, asthma, and anorexia and bulimia. The archive came to redefine and circulate his clients' knowledge as expert insider knowledge.

Epston realized that instead of seeing individual clients in individual sessions, he could take the problem resolution knowledges from one person and share them with another. These clients (at the time) never met face-to-face but were in touch with a rich reserve of wisdom and common experience with a common problem. Epston was able to patch together a network of clients with the purpose of consultation, information, and mutual support.[29] He called these client networks *leagues*. As the leagues grew, he realized that he had ready access to a wealth of insider consultants. His clients became his colleagues and consultants. The archive is now a vast offertory shared by Epston with people living around the world.

---

[28] In a conversation I had with Michael and David in 1995, they stated they had taken a rough poll of their clients' response to their letters. On average, the clients reported each letter was the worth of three sessions!

[29] With the onset of the digital age, David Epston is now able to transmit insider knowledge around the globe, and he does so on a daily basis (see Epston, 2009).

# THE ANTI-ANOREXIA/BULIMIA LEAGUE

In the mid-1990s, I was able to stretch and build on David Epston's league idea[30] and, together with a group of women (and their communities of concern) who were suffering/rediscovering their lives back from anorexia and bulimia, formed the Vancouver Anti-Anorexia/Bulimia League.[31] The novel difference, of course, was that we met with each other as a group and in person.

From its inception, this league offered a clear mandate for outspoken "insider" voices to be heard,[32] and quickly moved toward practices of public education and political activism (Vancouver Anti-Anorexia/Bulimia League, 1998). The Anti-Anorexia/Bulimia League uses an anti-language to

- establish a context in which women taken by anorexia/bulimia experience themselves as separate from the problem;
- view the person's body and relationships to others not as the problem—the problem is the problem (counters the effect of labeling, pathologizing, and totalizing descriptions);
- enable people to work together to defeat the complexities involved with the problem;
- consider the cultural practices of objectification used to objectify anorexia/bulimia instead of objectifying the woman as being anorexic/bulimic;
- relationally externalize the objectification of the problem that challenges the individualizing techniques of scientific classification and looks at the broader cultural and relational context for a more complete problem description;

---

[30] David Epston's anti-anorexia/bulimia ideas formed the foundation of the Vancouver Anti-Anorexia/Bulimia League. He also played an integral role in offering up ideas and support as the league was forming. He traveled a number of times from New Zealand to Vancouver, Canada, to meet and co-research with members of our league. Michael White also kept close tabs and would regularly send me his thoughts and questions regarding therapy and anorexia, the culture of the body and various poststructural writings.

[31] In general, leagues use an "anti-language" for explaining their philosophy and ideological position (e.g., the Anti-Depression and Anti-Anxiety Leagues). In doing so, league members act to externalize previously internalized problem discourse collectively.

[32] I presented many conference workshops alongside members of the league. On numerous occasions, league member therapists were in the professional audience listening to their past and present clients. Affording opportunities for a person's "status" to be raised from patient to consultant is primary in the work of narrative therapy.

- relationally externalize to introduce questions that encourage the persons taken by anorexia/bulimia to map the influence of the problem's devastating effects in their lives and relationships;
- relationally externalize to deconstruct the pathologizing "thingification" and objectification of women through challenging accepted social norms; and
- relationally externalize and thereby allow for the possibility of multiple descriptions and re-storying by bringing forth alternative versions of a person's past, present, and future.

The purpose of the Vancouver League (Madigan & Law, 1998a) was to traverse the questionable ideological and fiscal gaps that lay within the traditional treatment terrain of mental health. The league promoted the idea of independence and self-sufficiency. Its playing field was twofold: (a) preventive education through a call for professional and community responsibility and (b) an alternative and unconventional support system for those women caught between hospitals and community psychiatry.

Through regular meetings, league members, families, lovers, and friends took a direct action[33] approach to the problems of anorexia and bulimia. For example, through their development of a media watch committee, the league acted to publicly denounce pro-anorexic/bulimic activities against women's bodies through letters written to a wide variety of magazines, newspapers, and company presidents. This enabled the league to return the normative gaze through anti-anorexic/bulimic surveillance directed toward professional, educational, and consumer systems. The school action committee developed an anti-anorexic/bulimic program for primary and secondary school students; however, they found out that diets and concerns with body specification were now the talk of toddlers as young as 4 years of age. League T-shirts have the words "You are More Than a Body" emblazoned across the back, with the league name and logo printed on the front (they were always a hot-selling item). The league also held a candlelight vigil each year to honor their league friends who had died anorexic/bulimic deaths.

---

[33] Much to the delight of the membership, the league activities were highlighted in a 1995 *Newsweek* article on narrative therapy.

Radical in its philosophy, the Vancouver Anti-Anorexia/Bulimia League's mandate was to hold accountable those professional and consumer systems that knowingly render women with "eating disorders" dependent and marginalized. Dependency and marginalization can occur through practices of pathological classification; long-term hospitalization; medication; funding shortages; and messages of hopelessness, dysfunction, and blame.

The league's agenda was to win the "war" they believed was being waged on women's bodies on both the professional and community fronts. Through the process of reclaiming their lives from anorexia and bulimia, league members refused to accept the popular misconception that they alone were responsible for their so-called eating disorders. League members began to make a crucial shift in their identities from group therapy patients to community activists and insider consultants. In helping at the level of community, they were assisting other women and families and, in turn, helping themselves.

Given the choice of using a league member or another therapist for an anti-anorexic therapeutic reflecting team consultation, I always prefer, whenever possible, to access a league member. New clients struggling with disordered eating are always struck by the member's compassionate and direct reflections. It is common practice for us to pay ex-clients and league members to act as consultants to therapists in training and as reflecting team members.

## ANTI-ANOREXIA CO-RESEARCH

Below is an excerpt from a videotape that was made by a league member for the explicit purpose of circulating her ideas in the training of therapists on what they might need to know when working with the problem of anorexia and bulimia. This interview represents the narrative practice of using insider knowledge as co-research.

**Madigan:** What do therapists need to know when working with persons taken by anorexia and bulimia?

**Catherine:** Well, I guess that it's important that therapists know that anorexia and bulimia have to be dealt with on a number of different levels and that you can't just focus in on the individual. What's happening for them or what's happening in the family or what's happening in the environment or society is all important and all together. You have to deal with it on all levels, or else you're just dealing with just part of what the problem is, and I think it'll always come back if you don't.

**Madigan:** Is there anything that you have discovered that professionals do that is unhelpful in going free of bulimia and anorexia?

**Catherine:** Well, when they look at you as a bulimic person, you begin to look at yourself—entirely—that way too. You begin to identify purely with your anorexia and your bulimia and you lose yourself. You deny you have another aspect to yourself. You think about your eating disorder and everyone is saying well, "you're bulimic" or "you're anorexic" and anything you do wrong is attributed to you being a bulimic or anorexic. This way really denies them a lot, denies them their personhood. You could say that because I struggled with bulimia and anorexia once, but that's just one aspect of my life. I feel it gets really hard because you're trying so hard in the struggle to hold on to yourself, to the inner person, the person that needs to come out, and then when everyone is focusing just on the bulimia and your anorexia, the behavior, then they push you and yourself down. Every time people and professionals do that, you become smaller and smaller.

**Madigan:** What did you find helpful?

**Catherine:** I guess it had a lot to do with separating bulimia from myself. Being able to see it as one aspect of me and just that! And giving me my voice back, giving myself back my voice and pushing bulimia back, or trying to put bulimia back where it belongs; I don't know how to say that. Just trying to give it a sense of, I guess, separate yourself from it. You know, allow my voice to become louder and turning down the volume on the bulimic voice.

**Madigan:** Was there one tactic of bulimia that stands out for you as being particularly horrible?

**Catherine:** Well, yes, it was such a secretive thing. It told me that secrecy was the only way for me and it to survive. And I guess it caused me not only to have to keep it a secret to people on the outside, but it insisted I keep it a secret from everyone close around me and through this it imprisoned me. I couldn't reach out, I couldn't talk to people. And, as time goes on, you don't trust those people. Because it becomes your best friend. It's the only thing that made me feel better. Having a binge was to get rid of some of the rage by purging. It became everything. An all-purpose best friend, and coping mechanism, and it also kept me trapped and kept me doubting myself and the people around me.

**Madigan:** Is there anything that you have come up with to combat bulimia's compliance with secrecy?

**Catherine:** When I feel that it's trying to put a stranglehold of secrecy around me, I really actively think about it and say, okay, what am I doing? Am I isolating myself? Is the bulimia causing me to withdraw? Then turning down the volume and going, no, I'm not going to let it have control, and I actively really think of it as something separate. I call it for what it is and that's an abusive partner—it's just very abusive to me. By saying no to the abuse and reaching out for those people that are there, and have always really been there, really helps diminish its grip. The bulimia has kept me in prison and isolated me and denied me my own sense of self-worth and denied me the feeling that I am a good person and I am worth caring about and people do want to share and be a part of my life.

**Madigan:** I find your paralleling bulimia to that of an abusive relationship fascinating. Could you tell me more about this idea of yours?

**Catherine:** I was once writing a letter to my body and saying, "I'm sorry for all the abuse" and da, da, da, da and I really began to identify just how abusive bulimia is! And how it acts exactly like an abusive partner. It attacks me at the moment I'm most vulnerable, and it tries to keep me down. It tells me I'm no good. It tells me that no one else will like me and I can always depend on it and no one else will be as dependable. It tells me it's doing this because it really cares and it wants to do something really nice. You know, it finds all sorts of really insidious ways of destroying every sense of self and self-worth that you have. It keeps you distracted, and then it slowly abuses you physically and mentally. It keeps saying that "I care about you" and "nobody loves you like I do." That's what kept it so firmly planted in my life. When anyone disappointed me, even a little bit, I said, "Well, it's [bulimia] right." I am worthless, that's why this is happening, and I went to have a binge and yeah, it made me feel good for the short term, and you know I tried to nurture myself by filling myself up and get rid of the rage by purging. It did help in the short term, the very short term, but it has disastrous consequences.

**Madigan:** How did you manage to get free of bulimia's abuse?

**Catherine:** I think it was a number of things. First, the thing I really had to come to grips with was that it was an abusive relationship. Knowing about abusive relationships, I know it's not going to go away unless I get some help, right [laughs]. So, I really had to look at it, and whatever intellectual or emotional thing that kept me holding on to it had to go. I looked at it as separate from me, me in relation to an abusive partner, and I realized nothing was ever going to get better. I knew I would never gain control of it, that it doesn't really love me. That it really hates me and it has its own purpose and its own agenda, and that was to destroy me. And I had to really look at that and start letting go of all the lies that it had for keeping it in my life. And just like when you leave an abusive partner you have to reach out, I found there were some very persistent and good people, league people, positive people that where really working hard at letting me know that they where there, and they would be there. They were a heck of a lot better than a bulimic partner. Slowly, by just beginning to trust and realize, yes, they were there and they know me pretty well now.

**Madigan:** How did you put an end to the abusive relationship?

**Catherine:** I just kicked the bulimic bum out!

Is it any wonder that on viewing the league's "What Every Therapist Needs to Know About Anorexia and Bulimia, But Were Afraid to Ask" DVD,[34] the room of professionals and laypersons thundered with applause,

---

[34] Narrativetherapy.tv has extensive interview footage of consultations with Vancouver Anti-Anorexia/Bulimia League members.

interest, and tears? I asked psychiatrist Dr. Elliot Goldner, who at the time was the director of a hospital eating disorder program in Vancouver (and also a longtime friend), to offer his reflections after reading excerpts of the league's ongoing co-research project. Dr. Goldner wrote the following:

> The writings of the League underscore a potent fact; people struggling against anorexia and bulimia possess a wisdom and expertise that must not be marginalized. Their research is pulled from the pores of experience and has not been limited to eight hours a day, academic blinders, and political or financial motivations. To ignore their insight would be folly. Yet, psychiatry and therapy practices have too often disregarded such careful and painstaking research, and have preferred promises of quick fixes, and electrifying solutions from technology and scientism. (Madigan and Epston, 1995, p. 56)

When I listen, instead, to their words, these are some of the things I hear:

- Collaboration is helpful in fighting anorexia and bulimia; leagues such as the Vancouver Anti-Anorexia/Bulimia League can offer such collaboration.
- Anti-anorexic/bulimic actions help to combat eating disorders for individuals and societies; in contrast, nonaction (which characterizes some "therapy" or "support efforts") is not helpful.
- Empowerment of those persons fighting anorexia and bulimia is helpful in combating eating disorders; such empowerment is supported by respect and by separation of the person and the problem.
- Anorexia and bulimia can hold a person with the vice grip of an abusive partner; secrecy and shame can form the glue that adheres these problems to the person.
- Others (including those in "helping" professions) may worsen the problem; this often occurs when people confer certain knowledges about a person and constrain that person's identity and selfhood.

When we presented the league ideas in a public forum, we were continually reminded of their social impact on therapeutic possibilities. It is from within the wisdom of these co-research projects that therapists can be moved toward a reflexive accountability. We would argue that the weight of therapeutic accountability should be privileged and mediated through the knowledges of the once marginalized, not through a professionalized discourse (Madigan & Epston, 1995).

The league allowed for the distribution of client knowledge from one client to another. In addition, they often voiced strong opposition to those cultural and professional institutions that were problem supporting. The league's mandate was to undo the knotted dichotomy of difference, distance, and status presently wedged between psychologists/therapists and clients. The league could be seen as another step in stretching the ideas of transparency and reflecting teams (Epston, 1994; Madigan, 1991a) into the community.

The Vancouver Anti-Anorexia/Bulimia League encouraged a different kind of self-directed healing and encouraged persons to retrieve, and reflect on, what lay hidden in the wings of their imaginations. Members of the league realized that their ideas represented the tip of an untapped therapeutic iceberg.

# 5

# Evaluation

*The intellectual was rejected and persecuted at the precise moment*
*when the facts became incontrovertible, when it was forbidden*
*to say that the emperor had no clothes.*

—Michel Foucault

Psychologist Ian Parker (2008), who runs the Discourse Research Unit at the University of Manchester, summed up the dilemma of research for the narrative therapist quite nicely when he wrote the following:

> When we approach the concept of 'mental health' there is, of course, always a question in our minds; what is this 'mental health' that we intend to examine? These two words 'mental health' might, we think, be preferable to the couplet 'mental illness'; but, tempted as we might be to find some neutral terminology to approach this crucial research question, we know as qualitative researchers that every word we use is semiotically loaded, rich with meanings that will always locate words in discourses we may not want to endorse. We may, for example, want to avoid the notion that people who suffer distress are 'ill',

but the use of the term 'health' instead of 'illness' does not altogether escape medical discourse. And there still remain the problematic connotations of the term 'mental', for that presupposes that our objects of study are internal psychological states. Contemporary discourse is replete with words and images that locate the causes for our activities inside individual minds; we increasingly inhabit a 'psychological culture' that delimits the horizons of our inquiry. (p. 40)

If there was to be any interest and/or consistency between narrative therapy theory, practice, and research, the task of any research would be akin to that of the literary critic, insofar as cultural behavior can be treated only as a text that requires interpretation. This raises the important questions about the accuracy (or objectivity) of any research description.

I might suggest that therapeutic research interpretations are "fictions," but not in the sense that the events they describe did not happen. Rather, the interpretations are made and fashioned and, as such, are second- or even third-order accounts based on first-order communications of the person "being studied." Thus they are never definitive and can always be contested.

I would argue from a narrative therapy point of view that theory cannot be imposed onto therapeutic interview data, thereby rejecting any research that acts toward removing or avoiding this incompleteness (or contestability). For example, Geertz (1973) suggested that by turning culture into folklore and collecting it, they (psychology) turned cultures into traits and started counting it. And then they (psychology) turned culture into institutions and began classifying it, then turned it into structures and began to toy with it (Geertz, 1973, p. 29).

Renouncing grand psychological theories in favor of fine-grained interpretive explorations of the rich content of everyday life (through perhaps a method of ethnographic research[1]) would place the "native" actors'

---

[1] The practice of ethnography usually involves fieldwork in which the ethnographer lives among the population being studied. The ethnographer lives an ordinary life among the people, working with informants who are particularly knowledgeable or well placed to collect information. This fieldwork may last for extended period of time—usually over a year, and sometimes much longer. Although many people visualize ethnography as a field of study on "other" people and obscure tribes, many ethnographers work in quite familiar environments.

understanding of their actions at the forefront, and this understanding could tell us a little about how this particular person or family has come to respond to culture and how their lives work. Until very recently, not much research has been conducted on the practice of narrative therapy. This may be partially explained by narrative therapy practitioners moving away from anything they deemed scientific or methods that attempted to quantify lived experience. There is, however, an ever-increasing amount of "evidence" being collected as an argument for the effectiveness for narrative therapy practices.[2]

As a matter of "duty" (i.e., as a way to present a consistent structure for this American Psychological Association series book), I report on a few narrative therapy research projects in this chapter. The following synopsis on research comes from the Dulwich Centre website.[3]

Lynette Vromans (2008) investigated the process and outcome of narrative therapy for major depressive disorder in adults. The first objective of the research was to articulate a theoretical synthesis of narrative theory, research, and practice. The process of narrative reflexivity was identified as a theoretical construct linking narrative theory with narrative research and practice. The second objective was to substantiate this synthesis empirically by examining narrative therapy processes, specifically narrative reflexivity and the therapeutic alliance, and their relation to therapy outcomes. The third objective was to support the proposed synthesis of theory, research, and practice and provide quantitative evidence for the utility of narrative therapy by evaluating depressive symptoms and interpersonal relatedness outcomes through analyses of statistical significance, clinical significance, and benchmarking. To support this theoretical synthesis, a process–outcome trial evaluated eight sessions of narrative therapy for 47 adults with major depressive disorder. Dependent process variables were narrative reflexivity (assessed at Sessions 1 and 8) and therapeutic alliance (assessed

---

[2] This research section was put together through the assistance of David Denborough, the *International Narrative Therapy and Community Work Journal,* and Dulwich Centre Publications of Adelaide, South Australia.

[3] Reprinted from *Research, Evidence, and Narrative Practice,* by D. Denborough, November 2009, and retrieved from http://www.dulwichcentre.com.au/narrative-therapy-research.html. Copyright 2009 by the Dulwich Centre. Reprinted with permission.

at Sessions 1, 3, and 8). Primary dependent outcome variables were depressive symptoms and interpersonal relatedness. Primary analyses assessed therapy outcome at pretherapy, posttherapy, and 3-month follow-up and used a benchmarking strategy to evaluate pretherapy to posttherapy and posttherapy to follow-up gains, effect size, and pretherapy to posttherapy clinical significance. The clinical trial provided empirical support for the utility of narrative therapy in improving depressive symptoms and interpersonal relatedness from pretherapy to posttherapy, the magnitude of change indicating large effect sizes ($d = 1.10$–$1.36$) for depressive symptoms and medium effect sizes ($d = 0.52$–$0.62$) for interpersonal relatedness. Therapy was effective in reducing depressive symptoms in clients with moderate and severe pretherapy depressive symptom severity. Improvements in depressive symptoms, but not interpersonal relatedness, were maintained for 3 months following therapy. The reduction in depressive symptoms and the proportion of clients who achieved clinically significant improvement (53%) in depressive symptoms at posttherapy were comparable with improvements from standard psychotherapies, reported in benchmark research. This research has implications for assisting our understanding of narrative approaches, refining strategies that will facilitate recovery from psychological disorder, and providing clinicians with a broader evidence base for narrative practice.

David Besa (1994) evaluated narrative family therapy using single-system research designs. His study assessed the effectiveness of narrative therapy in reducing parent–child conflicts. Parents measured their child's progress by counting the frequency of specific behaviors during baseline and intervention phases. The practitioner–researcher used single-case methodology with a treatment package strategy, and the results were evaluated using three multiple baseline designs. Six families were treated using several narrative therapy methods including externalization, relative influence questioning, identifying unique outcomes and unique accounts, bringing forth unique redescriptions, facilitating unique circulation, and assigning between-session tasks. Compared with baseline rates, five of six families showed improvements in parent–child conflict, ranging from an 88% to a 98% decrease in conflict. Improvements occurred only when narrative therapy was applied and were not observed in its absence.

Mim Weber, Kierrynn Davis, and Lisa McPhie (2006) looked at narrative therapy, eating disorders, and groups in rural New South Wales, Australia. Their paper reported on a study conducted with seven women who identified themselves as experiencing depression as well as an eating disorder. Self-referred, the women participated in a weekly group for 10 weeks, with a mixture of topics, conducted within a narrative therapy framework. A comparison of pre- and postgroup tests demonstrated a reduction in depression scores and eating-disorder risk. All women reported a change in daily practices, together with less self-criticism. These findings were supported by a postgroup evaluation survey that revealed that externalization of, and disengagement from, the eating disorder strongly assisted the women to make changes in their daily practices. Although preliminary and short term, the outcomes of the present study indicate that group work conducted within a narrative therapy framework may result in positive changes for women entangled with depression and an eating disorder.

Fred W. Seymour and David Epston (1989) looked at an approach to childhood stealing. Childhood stealing is a distressing problem for families and may have wider community costs because childhood stealers often become adult criminals. This paper described a therapeutic "map" that emphasized direct engagement of the child, along with his or her family, in regarding the child from "stealer" to "honest person." Analysis of therapy with 45 children revealed a high level of family engagement and initial behavior change. Furthermore, a follow-up telephone call made 6 to 12 months after completion of therapy sessions revealed that 80% of the children had not been stealing at all or had substantially reduced rates of stealing.

Linzi Rabinowitz and Rebecca Goldberg (2009) examined an evaluation of an intervention using hero books to mainstream psychosocial care and support in South African schools via the curricula. They reported that hero books are a psychosocial support intervention developed by Jonathan Morgan (REPSSI), informed by narrative therapy ideas. This study presents preliminary evidence to support the contention that the mainstreaming of psychosocial support in the South African school curriculum by means of the hero book is likely to produce two significant outcomes:

1. Learners who have undergone the hero book process are more likely to perform better in the learning areas of life orientation and language (home language and first additional language) than learners whose educators did not use hero books, as measured by the same learning outcomes and assessment standards.

2. Learners whose educators used the hero book methodology to pursue academic outcomes are more likely to exhibit an improvement in their psychosocial well-being than learners whose educators did not use the hero book methodology. A mix of quantitative and qualitative data collection and analysis supports these findings. Although none of the findings are conclusive and the study admittedly has limitations, the strongest quantitative finding is this one: 77% of the learner's academic performance as measured by an average mark for all three learning areas (home language, first additional language, and life orientation) improved overall for the hero book group, as opposed to 55% for the control groups. This finding suggests that the hero book intervention might be pursued purely on its potential as a methodology to enhance academic learning outcomes and where any improvement in the psychosocial well-being of learners is an added bonus of the intervention. The sample size consisted of four control groups and four intervention groups across two research sites, the Western Cape and KwaZulu Natal. There were 172 learners in the control groups and 113 in the intervention groups.

Jane Speedy (with Gina Thompson and others; 2004) wrote an interesting paper titled "Living a More Peopled Life: Definitional Ceremony as Inquiry Into Psychotherapy 'Outcomes.'" This paper raised questions about the current European and North American culture of evidence-based practice and the conventions of "psychotherapy outcomes" research. Outsider witness practices and definitional ceremonies are suggested as collaborative research processes that sit more congruently with narrative, poststructuralist, and feminist ideas and with narrative therapy practices that may be equally effective ways of influencing policymakers and shaping future services. Narrative practitioners and the people consulting them are invited to contribute to an international narrative therapy outcomes research conversation.

Sonja Berthold's (2006) research focused on the Back From the Edge Project evaluation. This is an independent evaluation of a narrative therapy/collective narrative practice project conducted in two Aboriginal communities in Arnhem Land—Yirrkala and Gunyangara. The project aimed to (a) reduce suicidal thinking/behavior/injury, self-harm, and death by suicide; (b) enhance resilience, respect, resourcefulness, interconnectedness, and mental health of individuals, families, and communities and reduce prevalence of risk conditions; and (c) increase support available to individuals, families, and communities that have been affected by suicidal behaviors. The project was conducted as a partnership between Dulwich Centre and Relationships Australia Northern Territory. For more information about the project, see Denborough et al. (2006).

The independent evaluation found that the project worked because it (a) reminded people of their strength and their dreams; (b) increased the self-esteem and confidence of individuals and groups, and reinforced their ability to deal with suicide and suicidal thinking; (c) created an opportunity for these communities to forge links with another indigenous community, a link that strengthens and comforts both; (d) provided an audience for the stories and passed on the responses; (e) helped people see that their knowledge and experience is of value to others; (f) brought the community together to celebrate its strengths and abilities; (g) ensured that local workers were linked into and supporting this process; and (h) left a resource that is still being used.

A current research project by David Denborough (Dulwich Centre, Adelaide, South Australia) in collaboration with John Henley and Julie Robinson (Flinders University) examined the Tree of Life, a narrative therapy approach to responding to vulnerable children that was developed by Ncazelo Ncube (REPSSI) and David Denborough (Dulwich Centre). During 2009, the research project took place in two primary schools in South Australia to evaluate the effectiveness of the Tree of Life with children from refugee families. The data were analyzed and final results were made available in mid-2010.

# 6

# Future Developments

*Knowledge is not for knowing: Knowledge is for cutting.*
—Michel Foucault (*The Foucault Reader*)

The future of narrative therapy shines as bright as its remarkable history. Narrative therapy stands alone in its relational anti-individualist practice, and this seems to be finding a very large and ever-expanding worldwide audience. More and more therapists (from all the many disciplines of counseling) are turning to narrative's theory and practice as a way out of the heartless frontier that many psychologists describe. Psychology appears to want its life back from the limits that HMOs place on psychologists' practice and the emphasis on pharmacology and evidence-based practices.

I welcome all of you into the global community of narrative therapy.

## A FEW FUTURE CONSIDERATIONS

Michael White (2005) stated that "in most parts of the world that are experiencing the calamities associated with war, disease, displacement, and economic turmoil, children remain most acutely vulnerable to life-threatening hardship and trauma" (p. 24). It was his assertion that when working with young persons (anywhere) who were experiencing trauma, a great therapeutic importance should be placed on psychological, physical, and emotional safety so as to not retraumatize these children. He stated that it was through the furthering and developing of subordinate story lines, as stated within a narrative therapy framework of practice, that the child could be offered an "alternative territory of identity" to stand inside. It is within this safe standing place that the child begins to find unique and safe articulations on the experience of trauma.

Narrative therapy work with persons (children, adults, families, and communities) experiencing trauma does not require—as many theoretical practice orientations treating trauma might—that they speak directly (and immediately) to their experiences of trauma (and this does not mean that an importance is not placed on the re-telling). From a narrative therapy perspective, persons who cannot speak to these traumatic experiences (or do not feel safe enough to express their experiences) are not viewed as persons struggling under the influence of psychological mechanisms such as denial or suppression. In addition to this, the new and successful diagnosis of a posttraumatic stress disorder[1] is not explored or considered.

The imperative piece of this practice is to afford a clear statement of exception to the child or adult, offering the individual immunity from blame, guilt, shame, and so forth. Second, forcing out storied particulars of the trauma without considering numerous safety factors[2] would only act to re-traumatize the child and bring him or her closer to a renewed sense of unsafe vulnerability.

Finding ways to safely speak about trauma with an appreciated therapeutic acknowledgement and response to the child's reaction to trauma can

---

[1] In 2007 I was invited by my good friend Dr. Ed Mills—an eminent Canadian HIV and AIDS epidemiologist—on one of his countless working trips to Kampala, Mbale, and the displaced persons' camps a bit further north in Uganda. During this visit, I encountered countless discussions (and often a soft-handed ridicule aimed at all the "Western helpers") on the topic of the North American psychological notion known as *posttraumatic stress*. The local reply was always "Where is this 'post' you are referring to?"—a point well taken in Uganda and a point quite understandably misunderstood in the West.

[2] These include a wide-ranging discussion about their skills, knowledge, and abilities—discussing, for example, a child's or adult's skills in finding support in hostile contexts, finding methods of connecting with others to break the confines of isolation, and refusing to be included or a part of contexts that are reproducing of trauma.

bring forth powerful expressions about the trauma and a renewed hope for the child and his or her relationships. As the psychology of Western ideas wrongly finds its way to speak on behalf of the experience of other cultures (and begins to "treat" trauma throughout the developing world), Michael White's ideas become crucial. To wit, I am reminded of Just Therapy team member Taimalie Kiwi Tamasese's statement to me in 1991 that the last bastion of colonization in the world would be psychology.

Over the last few years, Cheryl White and David Denborough of the Dulwich Centre Foundation in Adelaide, South Australia, have been expanding on narrative therapy's work with children, families, and communities living within trauma (and their work extends to war-torn countries). They call this newly found work *collective narrative practices.*

Collective narrative practices involve work—designed in collaboration with colleagues from different parts of the world—with individuals, groups, and communities who have endured significant hardship. Taking narrative therapy principles and practices specific to trauma (as developed by Michael White and David Epston) as the starting point, their cross-cultural partnerships have resulted in the development of a diverse range of collective narrative methodologies. They include

- collective timelines,
- maps of history,
- collective narrative documentation,
- story lines that link individuals/communities through the exchanging of messages,
- songs of sustenance,
- narrative checklists of social and psychological resistance,
- the Tree of Life—a collective narrative approach to working with vulnerable children,
- the Team of Life—offering young people a sporting chance, and
- the Kite of Life—strengthening relations across generations in immigrant/refugee communities.

The collective practice team has worked collaboratively with individuals in prisons who have been subjected to sexual violence, Australian Aboriginal communities, vulnerable children in Southern Africa, and genocide survivors in Rwanda. Collective narrative practices are culturally respectful, resonant, and effective when working with children and adults who have experienced significant trauma or adversity. To date, the collective narrative practice teams have worked in Australia, Rwanda, Israel, Russia, East Timor, Uganda, Bosnia, Palestine, and elsewhere.

As a result of its attention to ethics and social justice, to anti-individualism, and to a practice respecting of the wider social and political contexts on the shaping of cultural identity, narrative therapy is rapidly expanding around the world. It is securing large therapeutic followings in places like South Africa, sub-Saharan Africa, China, Japan, Mexico, Russia, and India. At the moment, the places that appear to be experiencing the swiftest rise and interest in narrative therapy are Hong Kong, Singapore, Brazil, and South Korea.

Canada and the Scandinavian countries have some of the best social support networks in the word today, and it only makes sense that these countries have a very long-standing and ever-growing large narrative therapy tradition. In countries like Ireland and France, people are just discovering narrative's practice merit, and a few institutes of learning are being set up.

The rate of growth continues to be slower in the United States, although there are long-standing narrative therapy communities in Boston, Miami, Minneapolis, New York, San Francisco, and Seattle. This slower growth may be a result of the practice of psychology swinging (through its institutions) to the right (although recent shifts on health care may, I hope, prove me wrong). From what I read and hear from my American colleagues, this right-leaning movement in mental health care appears to be pushing most psychological services to the brink of despair and to what my American colleague Bill Madsen called *institutionalized dysfunction*. As a result, it might become more difficult to find the commitment to helping others when the helping organizations in charge of helping are (necessarily) in desperate need of help.

More than in most countries, in the United States accountants have been placed in charge of mental health policy (I could only imagine if psychologists were placed in charge of American monetary policy!). These money managers for the predominant HMOs are clearly doing what they are mandated to do: make money.

The very idea of making money on the "backs" of an American public mental health clientele/system appears unethical, but nevertheless in a free-market economy these managers have the right to advertise their companies as savvy buys on the New York Stock Exchange, which they do. Mental health HMO stocks, in case we forget, are set up (and legally bound) to act in the best interests of the shareholder. Therefore, mental health stocks have set out a business plan designed to offer clients less therapeutic services as a way to satisfy a shareholder agreement to do everything possible to make their profits higher.

Working alongside and buttressing this mental health care-less money-making plan is a pharmaceutical industry that "fixes" America's mental woes by offering up low-cost chemical pills to assist with each person's HMO-mandated *Diagnostic and Statistical Manual of Mental Disorders* diagnosis. Without too much study or consideration, the marriage between HMOs and big pharmacology is a truly remarkable mental health care business opportunity. And despite its rough-hewn ethics and the fact that it comes at a very steep cost to those who are struggling and vulnerable, it is honest in what it sets out to do. So whatever you might feel regarding the use of psychological capitalism and its exploitation of clients (and their psychologists, mental health workers, and social workers), it is proving to be an unquestioned business model of great reward, and as a result, this model is clearly here to stay.

With a strong psychological capitalist plan in place, it is not too difficult to see why a narrative therapy practice with a poststructural history and its anti-individualist mandate might not be readily accepted at certain American boardroom tables. However, despite these corporate mental health conditions, American-styled narrative therapists, (almost all) graduate schools of mental health learning, and numerous big city agencies are, more than ever, doing their utmost to incorporate narrative ideas as a means to best serve their clients. These American professionals find a way to do this with a great and unbridled commitment, despite the most egregious corporate working conditions known to psychology in the Western world.

David Epston's primary work these days involves a co-researching of co-research with insiders and their knowledge (a second-order co-research). This model of practice finds a congruent fit with poststructural ideas (and how working in conjunction with insiders has rich historical traditions within narrative therapy). More and more insider leagues and co-research are beginning and will be central to our future work. Epston (1998, 2009) is currently taking his co-research idea into many different domains and exploring the numerous possibilities of this work. What follows is a brief excerpt/transcript of his recent co-research with a client named Julie, in which he revisits the questions he once asked her during their therapy sessions and calls on her knowledge for further explanation and understanding of the initial questions.

**David:** Julie, had anorexia up until then insisted you were both unworthy of and unacceptable to the very living of your life?

**Julie:** This question intrigued me as it shifted the focus from myself to anorexia. It raised the possibility that my feelings of unworthiness and unacceptability were not necessarily indicative of any essential or fundamental attributes of "me-ness" but were maybe something altogether different. To consider anorexia/bulimia as an agent of insistence, its argument having such power to make me "know" beyond doubt that I was unworthy, was challenging and stimulated a conceptual upheaval and consequent shift in my thinking. A/b's [anorexia/bulimia's] power of persuasion was evident when I realized that the feelings of unworthiness didn't seem the result of insistence but were experienced by me as irrefutable "facts"—facts chameleon-like in their ability to blend into every cell of my body and mind so as their infiltration went unnoticed. Being unaware of this infiltration, every small gesture of life seemed to demand an apology—an apology for still living despite my unworthiness, an apology that was never enough. To live so apologetically while still holding on to what felt like a desperate desire to be acceptable to life and love was a painful existence. I experienced a pressure that I was meant to relinquish the living of my life as the best apology, and therefore any signs of life could be seen as a punishable deviation.

**David:** Julie, from anorexia's immoral perspective, were you incited to execute yourself as your one remaining moral act?

**Julie:** I was shocked by this question, even though I was becoming familiar with the challenges I experienced when considering David's questions and the depth of thought and emotion they provoked. They took me to the heart of experiences in my life that had been shamefully buried. These experiences may have remained buried until this dialogue encouraged me to unearth and voice them; discovering a flow of words like tears, tears of sadness and relief at being able to finally find a voice I had forgotten; a cascade of words of excitement, recognition and also grief at being able to see and re-experience and tell my life in new and surprising ways; a rambling of words as I took a round-about time and way to find my way to an answer, like a rambling rose reaching out to its flowering; tendrils of words: tentative. Words free to be spoken for the first time. I wish I could say I spoke unapologetically, but in those early days of conversation about a/b I felt I was breaking all of a/b's rules and so inviting its wrath. I felt guilty for speaking, fraudulent and unqualified. I felt exposed and continued to apologize, but David was always generous and patient in his reassurance and encouragement. I had never been asked before about my experience of a/b. Now someone was asking and also listening. I cannot underestimate the role this took in changing my life.

## DEVELOPING IDEAS IN NARRATIVE THERAPY

My longtime friend Bill Madsen of Cambridge, Massachusetts, is one of the many future-thinking narrative therapists working through pronarrative practice methods with numerous mental health organizations. These organizations, from public mental health clinics to child protection and welfare agencies, maintain a deep desire to really help people. Bill has developed ways to initiate narrative ideas into institutional paper work, staff supervision, policy and agency-wide consultations and meetings, etc. He has also advanced a new therapist/worker language to combat psychological practices that are perpetually stuck inside so-called best-practice models and evidence-based research nonsense. He has recently written a second edition of *Collaborative Therapy With Multi-Stressed Families* (Madsen, 2007), which I highly recommend to all social service providers.

I also value the ongoing theoretical work of narrative therapist and author Jon Winslade (2009). He is currently articulating an attractive case for integrating the work of the poststructural French philosopher Gilles Deleuze into narrative practice. Specifically, he is interested in how Deleuze builds on Foucault's concepts of power and represents these power relations diagrammatically in terms of lines of power. Deleuze, Winslade explained, is a philosopher "of becoming," which connects with narrative therapy's inquiries toward preferred lives and lifestyles. Deleuze asked the simple question, "How might one live?"—with the focus on creative possibility.

Other work I have my eye on includes Devon MacFarland's work in Vancouver, British Columbia, Canada, and David Nylund's[3] and Julie Tilsen's work (in Winnipeg, Manitoba, Canada, and in Sacramento, California, respectively) with transgendered persons. I see their practice ideas and writing on the forefront of therapeutic discussions regarding identity, gender, and the opposition to binary descriptions of personhood.

My colleague and good friend Vikki Reynolds[4] instituted a practice of worker solidarity groups (particularity with marginalized workers who are working with marginalized populations experiencing horrendous conditions for living). Her group work acts to form therapeutic practices congruent within an ethical activist center. Vikki's work is expanding and developing in generative ways, and I look forward to witnessing more of this solidarity work.

My long-time collaborator and good friend Ian Law has a new work in discursive therapies that expands on narrative therapy theory. Ian's latest projects will push us deeper into poststructuralism and the work of Michel Foucault. We look forward to his book release through Routledge.

Australian Alan Jenkins's (2009) work in trauma and abuse expands on his ethical invitational model of narrative practice. His latest book *Becoming Ethical: A Parallel Political Journey With Men Who Have Abused* is worth reading and rereading. There is also much newly inspired work in this same area of trauma and abuse by New Zealander Johnella Bird;

---

[3] David Nylund has been a faculty member of the Vancouver School for Narrative Therapy since 2007.

[4] Vikki Reynolds has been a faculty member of the Vancouver School for Narrative Therapy since 2005.

Alan Wade[5] in Duncan, Canada; and Cathy Richardson in Victoria, Canada.

As I meet more and more narrative therapists from around the world, I see a (welcomed) desire to move toward more creative explorations within the craft of narrative therapy. David Epston and the faculty at our Vancouver School for Narrative Therapy are excited about the possibilities of spearheading a return to our innovative past, when therapy training was about creativity, apprenticeship, invention, skill development, and rigorous study.

The Vancouver School for Narrative Therapy begins a new Intercontinental Studies program in narrative therapy in fall 2010 (http://www.therapeuticconversations.com). The schooling and meticulously designed narrative therapy study program encourages training conversations we call *reverberating apprenticeships* (D. Epston, personal communication, 2009). These reverberating apprenticeships will take place within all levels of our training and supervision programs and involve insider teachers, live session trainings, reading groups, and ethnographic group co-research work (Tyler, 1990). The Vancouver School for Narrative Therapy envisions the reverberating apprenticeships as a collaborative method of training designed to bring forth more narrative inventiveness to our teaching and ongoing clinical practice. Our commitment is to train therapists in the intimate particularities and nuances toward becoming dynamic, confident, and creative practitioners.

We have only just scratched the tip of the creative iceberg in what might be possible in narrative therapy. Adopting a posture of narrative inventiveness returns narrative therapists back toward the collaborative and creative spirit of our therapy work—back to Dulwich Centre Publications' production of the *Collected and Selected Papers,* and forward toward insider ethnographies (and staying up late designing therapeutic questions to match the politics of poststructural ideas). Narrative therapy's inventiveness encourages a comeback toward viewing narrative therapy as a craft and moves away from the stale guidelines of a map-making technician.

---

[5] For great live interviews/conversations between Alan Wade and Johnella Bird on the topics of abuse and trauma, go to http://www.therapeuticconversations.com.

Narrative therapy continues to step toward the exciting ideas of insider knowledge, viewing this as a separate and unique discourse (Madigan & Epson, 1995) and set apart from expert knowledge, a discourse that is preferred in the advancement of narrative practice knowledge. When I, David Epson, Lorraine Grieves, and (numerous) members of the Vancouver Anti-Anorexia/Bulimia League were organizing community gatherings and producing insider documents back in the 1990s, we simply thought it was the smartest thing to do. We thought communalizing our efforts was the smartest therapeutic tack to take because women were dying and jumping off bridges and struggling inside isolated hospital rooms. Leagues and collections of insider knowledges acted in opposition to the problems preference of isolation—simple enough. They still do.

Communities of concern were designed to help people step their lives back from the death throes of anorexia and bulimia and toward health (and preferred lives) through their enduring connections within these communities of concern. It was within these gatherings (and the actions that followed, in part, on account of these gatherings) that problem identities morphed and changed into knowledged and consultant identities. Aaron Monroe and Sean Spear of Vancouver, British Columbia, Canada, are currently developing communities of concern and insider knowledge documents that are shaping policy and garnering program research and development money. Their narrative therapy work is on the front lines of Canada's poorest urban neighborhood, working narratively with a diverse population of persons struggling with homelessness, mental health issues, and drug and alcohol use (Waldegrave, 1996).

Aaron and Sean's community-inspired insider "shelter folk"[6] meetings (S. Speer, personal communication, 2010) not only are hugely inspirational but also act as the primary language and knowledge used when writing new grant proposals for shelter programs, needle exchange programs, and so on. Insider knowledge is also used when addressing the issues of shelter rules, ethical guidelines, insider drug use, professional

---

[6] Sean Speer invented the term *shelter folk* as a way to psychologically and geographically rename and relocate the person away from a homeless identity—and all the harm and taken-for-granted meaning that this name inscribes.

conduct, staff meetings, family and community involvement, work programs, etc. These insider gatherings place the insider's knowledge into direct action. They excite a preferred difference among the so-called chronic identities that have created this knowledge and hopefully inspire change in the professional groups who initially named them *chronic.*

During my recent marathon visits with David Epston in 2009, we spent the majority of our time speaking about the implications of critical ethnography in our work. The area of critical ethnography is by no means new to narrative therapy practice and affords our practice a well-researched discipline and methodology for insider collaboration. A critical ethnographic practice in narrative therapy would use the privilege and skills made available to professionals to penetrate the borders and silences that keep the voice of the client and his or her insider knowledge barricaded and unknown.

Critical ethnography is important to the narrative practitioner because it resists a domestication of the subject (and/or the therapeutic process). By resisting domestication, it moves us from asking "what is" to "what could be" (Madison, 2005). By this I mean that the practice of a narrative ethnographic therapy would disrupt the status quo by unsettling both the neutrality of language and any taken-for-granted assumptions of power and control.

The ongoing future of narrative practice appears to be founded in our continuing desire to collaborate in authentic (rather than token) ways with the people who come to see us in therapy each day. This would bring forth an increased investment in the collegial value we place on our clients and produce our co-presenting, writing, and researching together as normal practice. In addition, more robust collaborations would mean attempting more initiatives to fully appreciate, explore, and bring public recognition to the insider knowledge cultures we work with. Cultures could include refugees; transgendered persons; parents who stay at home minding children; children diagnosed with attention-deficit disorder and Asperger's syndrome; persons without homes; youth who run away; and people struggling with relationships to drug use, eating disorders, corporate anxiety, suburban sadness, couple unrest, and the full range of experiences from simply living among our cultures.

# 7

# Summary

Poststructural ideas and narrative therapy raise some of the most potent therapeutic questions we are capable of phrasing. Whatever voice the field of psychology warrants, narrative therapy will continue to push the field toward a consideration of poststructuralism, anti-individualism, social justice, and critical ethnography—in all its forms. In doing so, narrative therapy will continue to shake the field loose from preconceptions regarding "normal" ways of performing therapy, supervision, and research.

One day in 1991, Michael White was piloting his plane high in the skies above Adelaide, South Australia. After he had successfully shown me his deft ability to fly like a bird by using only the warm air updrafts to climb higher, he turned and said, "You know, Stephen, I've always found that the people we work with are far more interesting than they let on." I wondered if he was saying something about the need for therapists to view a person's life story as much more interesting than the story being told. Perhaps this small practice of appreciation is our primary job as therapists—to help people re-remember, reclaim, and re-invent a richer, thicker, and more meaningful alternative story.

In the aftermath of Michael White's death, I remember him forever reminding me that narrative therapy was—first and foremost—a therapy of appreciation, a privileged conversational appreciation of a person's lived experience, know-how, skills, abilities, etc. Michael's version of narrative therapy was nothing less than a complete celebration of the other. This was his practice legacy—with friends, therapists, and clients alike.

Michael also had an unwavering commitment to the simple idea of anti-individualism. For Michael, to address a person's struggles in therapy without a relational and contextual understanding of lived experience was utterly and entirely absurd. For him, psychology's foundation within individualist ideas represented a disembodied and disconnected sense of "reality"—one that fell short of explaining the wonder and splendor of human experience.

The practices of individualism within therapy, in all its various and wide-sweeping forms, truly saddened Michael. He recognized that individualism was not just a theoretical debate and felt that the practice of individualist ideas in therapy created long-lasting negative distress in our communities (and in both therapists' and clients' lives and relationships).

People tell me (fairly regularly) in therapy that their prior experience of being "treated" with drugs, misrepresented in file notes, "wrongly" inscribed with a diagnosis,[1] and engaged in "somewhat boring" therapeutic conversations was not all that helpful. Some people express a great sorrow about the therapeutic relationship, and others tell me how bitter they've become on account of psychological "treatment."

People's expressions about their negative therapeutic experiences may not be surprising to many of you. But despite client claims and protests, the dominant practice mode of therapy treatment remains the same. The clients' warning is that professional expertise is becoming somewhat deaf to their experience. This growing and censured deafness within therapy is both depressing and curious. Depression about professional deafness in a listening field speaks for itself. The curiosity is situated in the articulations

---

[1]To be transparent, in all of my years as a practicing therapist, I have never participated in conducting a *Diagnostic and Statistical Manual of Mental Disorders* diagnosis. This may be in part because of working in our Canadian mental health system and my training as a narrative therapist early on in my career.

of so many psychologists I meet and train who articulate how they also feel that no one is listening to their experience in therapy.

Psychologists are heard saying (and writing) how frustrated they are in not being allowed to help clients in "better ways" (than they currently are). Many psychologists today are complaining about the futility of having to train so hard to get licensure, only to end up not being able to fully use their "skills of helping." For example, they complain about being mandated to diagnose people in order to get paid (whether they believe in the diagnosis or not) and pressured by the limited number of sessions of therapy they can offer their clients.

I've often wondered if both clients and therapists state a preference for the therapeutic experience of the other to be different (perhaps more profound and intimate, or perhaps a tad more useful), then what would they have to do—collaboratively—to figure out a way to remove what is standing in their way? Whatever the answer to this question might be (depending on where you live, the privilege you have, and who you work for), I'm certain an answer can be found.

I tell psychologists in training that the cavalry is *not* coming. I tell them that they are officially on their own (alongside their clients and supportive colleagues) to help initiate change. But once they close their office door, they are free to perform and participate in all sorts of beautiful, compassionate, and wildly engaging therapeutic discussions (because the institution has not yet found a way to take the marvel of the helping relational experience entirely away).

So in some ways, as sad and rotten as it is sometimes for people on both sides of the therapeutic table, it really doesn't matter if the helping solutions of mainstream psychology have actually become the problem. One can always resist the practice of being unhelpful by learning and reading more, forming supportive collectives with other therapists and insiders, and finding ways to take up new and more helpful ways of practice.

As a first step, it is crucial to view a client's insider knowledge as novel (and not as a complaint, or as problematic, or as a form of "therapeutic resistance"). And one way of encouraging this is to begin a committed dialogue toward openly listening and situating what clients are saying about problems, culture, and the process of therapy. Once our profession begins to listen to the people who come to see us, and less to our professional selves and fossilized theories, I wonder how we might begin to view ourselves and what we might do in therapy a little bit differently. I wonder if hope and possibility might spring forth in our work and if this would grow us larger or smaller.

Finally, I wonder what it would take for all of us involved in the helping professions to consider this practice we call *therapy* as our life's work—considering what we do as a labor of love. This may help us acknowledge how entirely blessed and privileged we are to be afforded the opportunity to do this work. And if helping people was measured as our life's work, I wonder if we would figure out more respectful ways of helping the people we serve (and ourselves). I wonder where these new therapeutic practices and commitments about helping people might bring us. And I wonder where they might step us toward.

# Glossary of Key Terms

ALTERNATIVE STORIES    Therapists will often interact with numerous overwhelmingly thin conclusions and problem stories told by the people who come to see them in therapy. Narrative therapists are more interested in conversations that seek out alternative stories, which are identified by the person in therapy as stories that they would like to live their lives through. The therapist is interested in creating sustainable conversations supporting preferred stories of identity that assist people to break from the influence of the problems they are facing.

ANTI-INDIVIDUALISM    Modern psychology is based in individualism; narrative therapy is based in anti-individualism. Contemporary philosophy is dominated by anti-individualism, which holds that a person's thoughts, meaning, expression, and so on are relational responses to a cultural context and not determined by what is a priori "inside the person's head." The fact that a person's utterances and thoughts have a certain content and refer to certain things, states, or events in the world is determined not only by the person's brain state but also by his or her relations to the linguistic community, dominant norms, and physical environment.

ARCHIVE    This is a technical term Foucault (1972) used in *The Archaeology of Knowledge.* It designates the collection of all material traces left behind by a particular historical period and culture.

BODY    Narrative therapy is particularly concerned with the relations between political power and the body and analyzes various historical ways of training the body to make it socially productive. The body is an element to be managed in relation to strategies of the economic and social management of populations. This body description is the one taken up by the Vancouver Anti-Anorexia/Bulimia League.

CRITICAL ETHNOGRAPHY    Critical ethnography is a perspective through which a researcher can ask questions. It attempts to free researchers from ideologies that detract from informed reportage. Critical ethnography adopts a complex theoretical orientation toward culture, which—in collectives of differing magnitude, whether educational institutions, student communities, classrooms, etc.—is treated as heterogeneous, conflictual, negotiated, and evolving, as distinct from unified, cohesive, fixed, and static. Also, in contrast with a relativistic view of cultures as different but equal, critical ethnography explicitly assumes that cultures are positioned unequally in power relations. Critical ethnography is related to critical theory.

COMMUNITY OF DISCOURSE    A *discourse community* can be defined as people who share similar thoughts and ideas. The fan base of the Rolling Stones, for example, might constitute a discourse community. Within this fan base, certain attitudes would be considered unacceptable and outside of the community. For example, someone who does not hold the song "Brown Sugar" in the same high esteem as other members of the discourse community might be summarily "tossed out on his ear." Ideology defines what can be discussed.

CULTURAL HEGEMONY    Cultural hegemony is the philosophic and sociological concept, originated by the Marxist philosopher Antonio Gramsci, that a culturally diverse society can be ruled or dominated by one of its social classes. Cultural hegemony is the dominance of one social group over another—for example, the ruling class over all other classes. The theory states that the ideas of the ruling class come to be viewed as the norm and are seen as universal ideologies that benefit everyone, although they really only benefit the ruling class.

DECENTERED THERAPEUTIC POSTURE  The term *decentered* in narrative therapy does not refer to the intensity of the therapist's engagement (emotional or otherwise) with people seeking consultation, but rather to the therapist's achievement in according priority to the personal stories and to the knowledges and skills of these people. People have a "primary authorship" status in therapy, and the knowledges and skills that have been generated in the history of their lives are the principal considerations.

DECONSTRUCTION  Deconstruction is an approach introduced by French philosopher Jacques Derrida. It may be used in therapy, philosophy, literary analysis, or other fields. Deconstruction generally tries to demonstrate that any text (story) is not a discrete whole but contains several irreconcilable and contradictory meanings; that any text, therefore, has more than one interpretation; that the text itself links these interpretations inextricably; that the incompatibility of these interpretations is irreducible; and thus that an interpretative reading cannot go beyond a certain point. Paul Ricoeur is another prominent supporter and interpreter of Derrida's philosophy. He defined deconstruction as a way of uncovering the questions behind the answers of a text or tradition.

DEFINITIONAL CEREMONY  The definitional ceremony metaphor structures the therapeutic arena as a context for the rich description of people's lives, identities, and relationships. White used the definitional ceremony metaphor from the work of Barbara Myerhoff (1982, 1986), a cultural anthropologist.

DISCIPLINE  Discipline is a mechanism of power that regulates the behavior of individuals in the social body. This is done by regulating the organization of space (e.g., architecture), of time (e.g., timetables), and of people's activity and behavior (e.g., drills, posture, movement). It is enforced with the aid of complex systems of surveillance. Foucault emphasized that power is not discipline; rather, discipline is simply one way in which power can be exercised.

DISCOURSE  This book uses the term *discourse* to mean what gets to be said and who gets to say it and with what authority. However, the term *discourse* has several definitions. Sociologists and philosophers tend to use the term to describe the conversations and the meaning behind them by a group of people who hold certain ideas in common. Such is the definition by philosopher Michel Foucault, who held discourse to be the acceptable statements made by a certain type of discourse community.

DISCURSIVE PRACTICE   Discursive practices are all the ways that a culture creates social and psychological realities. This term refers to a historically and culturally specific set of rules for organizing and producing different forms of knowledge. It is not a matter of external determinations being imposed on people's thought; rather, it is a matter of rules that, like the grammar of a language, allow certain statements to be made.

EXPERIENCE   Experience can be defined as an interrelation between knowledge, types of normativity, and forms of subjectivity in a particular culture at a particular time.

EXTERNALIZING   White and Epston observed that therapeutic progress was enhanced when the therapist and person were able to talk about the problem in a more relational and contextualized way. Narrative therapy uses a method of externalizing problems to bring forth possible re-descriptions and the chance for clients to reposition themselves with the problem. The identity of the described problem is viewed as separate from the identities of the person. In this process, the problem becomes a separate relational entity within a context of power/knowledge and thus external to the person or relationship that was ascribed as the problem. Those problems that are considered to be "inherent," as well as those relatively fixed qualities that are attributed to persons and to relationships, are rendered less fixed and less restricting. Externalizing of the problem enables persons to separate from the dominant stories that have been shaping their lives and relationships. Externalizing is by no means a "requirement" of narrative therapy and represents one option within a range of narrative practices.

GENEALOGY   Michel Foucault's concept of genealogy is the history of the position of the subject, which traces the development of people and society (in this case, narrative therapy questions, ideas, concepts) through history.

HETERONORMATIVITY This is a term for a set of lifestyle norms that hold that people fall into distinct and complementary genders (male and female) with natural roles in life. It also holds that heterosexuality is the normal sexual orientation and states that sexual and marital relations are most (or only) fitting between a man and a woman. Consequently, a "heteronormative" view is one that promotes alignment of biological sex, gender identity, and gender roles with what is now called "the gender binary."

IDEOLOGY Ideology translates to the science or study of ideas. However, ideology tends to refer to the way in which people think about the world and their ideal concept of how to live in the world. For example, in U.S. politics, the term *ideology* may separate the difference between Democrat and Republican, and those sharing the ideology of one group over another are likely to vote accordingly. Usually a culture has multiple political ideologies, with some less popular than others. Many have difficulty seeing past the two competing ideologies to examine other political ideologies present in the culture. For example, few Libertarians, Green Party members, or Peace and Freedom ideologists are elected, because most voters think in terms of Democrat and Republican candidates only.

INDETERMINACY Indeterminacy is in the subjunctive mood because it is that which is not yet settled, concluded, or known. It is all that may be, might be, could be, perhaps even should be. The underlying quality of social life should be considered to be one of theoretical absolute indeterminacy. The relation of indeterminacy to the subjunctive mood is also discussed by J. Bruner (1986).

INSTITUTIONS Foucault noted that institutions are a way of freezing particular relations of power so that a certain number of people are advantaged.

KNOWLEDGE PRACTICE A knowledge practice viewed as "truth" within a cultural discourse sets standards for the specifications of the individual, around which the individual shapes his or her life.

LANDSCAPE OF ACTION    Landscape of action questions center on events that happened in a person's telling of their lives and links these events through time, forming a plot line. These questions are organized through events, circumstance, sequence, time, and plot.

LANDSCAPE OF IDENTITY    Landscape of identity questions are (in part) those regarding what the client might conclude about the action, sequences, and themes described in response to the landscape of action questions. Landscape of identity questions also bring forth relevant categories addressing cultural identities, intentional understandings, learnings, and realizations. Nonessentialism: The concept of nonessentialism was famously expanded on by Michel Foucault (1984a) in his *History of Sexuality,* in which he argued that even gender and sexual orientation are contrived formations and that our concept of essentialist notions of gender or sexuality is flawed. For example, he argued that the entire class of homosexuality is, in fact, quite recent, built up by cultural norms and an interplay between different groups in society, but with no more essential a quality than, for example, the idea of beauty.

NORMAL AND THE PATHOLOGICAL NORMALIZATION    Contemporary society is a society based on medical notions of the norm, rather than on legal notions of conformity to codes and the law. Hence criminals need to be "cured" of a disease, not punished for an infraction of the law. There is an insoluble tension between a system based on law and a system based on medical norms in our legal and medical institutions.

PERFORMANCE    When discussing the performance aspects of ritual process, Turner (1980) suggested that performance literally means to furnish completely or thoroughly. To perform is thus to bring something about; to consummate something; or to carry out a play, order, or project. But in the carrying out, one holds something new may be generated. The performance transforms itself.

POSTMODERNISM    In critical theory and philosophy, postmodernism serves as a striking counterpoint to classical foundations of philosophy. Although earlier philosophers and theorists were devoted to the ongoing exploration of a universal system, postmodernists focused on the role of that search in creating what is known as truth itself. To most postmodernist theorists, it is the discourse itself that gives rise to any sort of perceived universality.

POSTSTRUCTURALISM    Poststructuralism grew as a response to structuralism's perceived assumption that its own system of analysis was somehow essentialist. Poststructuralists hold that, in fact, even in an examination of underlying structures, a slew of biases introduce themselves, on the basis of the conditioning of the examiner. At the root of poststructuralism is the rejection of the idea that there is any truly essential form to a cultural product, as all cultural products are by their very nature formed and therefore artificial.

POWER/KNOWLEDGE    One of the most important features of narrative therapy is that mechanisms of power produce different types of knowledge, which collate information on people's activities and existence. The knowledge gathered in this way further reinforces exercises of power. The use of the *Diagnostic and Statistical Manual of Mental Disorders* and client files are examples of these techniques as a form of social control. Foucault's work cautions that what we may take to be knowledge may instead be nothing more than powerful concepts perpetuated by authorities, and those concepts may change our understanding of ourselves and our world.

POWER    Power is not a thing but a relation, power is not simply repressive but also productive, and power is not simply a property of the state. Power is not something that is exclusively localized in government and the state (which is not a universal essence). Rather, power is exercised throughout the social body. Power operates at the most micro levels of social relations. Power is omnipresent at every level of the social body.

RE-AUTHORING CONVERSATIONS    Re-authoring conversations reinvigorate people's efforts to understand what is happening in their lives, what has happened, how it has happened, and what it all means. In this way, these conversations encourage a dramatic re-engagement with life and with history and provide options for people to more fully inhabit their lives and their relationships. Questions are introduced that encourage people to generate new proposals for action, accounts of the circumstances likely to be favorable to these proposals for action, and predictions about the outcome of these proposals.

RE-MEMBERING CONVERSATIONS   Re-membering conversations are not about passive recollection but about purposive engagements with the significant figures of one's history and with the identities of one's present life who are significant or potentially significant. These figures and identities do not have to be directly known in order to be identified as significant to persons' lives.

RE-STORYING   The therapeutic notion of re-storying creates the possibility that change is always possible. Therefore, any totalized description of a person's past, present, or future can be reconfigured, recollected, and re-remembered differently.

SELF   Although different poststructural thinkers' views on the self vary, the self under study is said to be constituted by discourse(s). Narrative therapy's approach to the self stretches out beyond the more popular and/or generalized accounts of who persons are (e.g., dominant and/or individualized categories of personhood) and of who persons are stated or labeled to be by the expert of psychological knowledge.

SOCIAL CONSTRUCTIONISM   A major focus of social constructionism is to uncover the ways in which individuals and groups participate in the creation of their perceived social reality. It involves looking at the ways social phenomena are created, institutionalized, and made into tradition by humans. A socially constructed reality is one that is seen as an ongoing, dynamic process that is reproduced by people acting on their interpretations and their knowledge of it.

STORY   Stories determine the meaning given to experience. Stories enable persons to link aspects of their experience through the dimension of time (past/present/future). There does not appear to be any other mechanism for the structuring of experience that so captures the sense of lived time or that can adequately represent the sense of lived time. It is through stories that we obtain a sense of our lives changing. It is through stories that we are able to gain a sense of the unfolding of the events of our lives through recent history, and it appears that this sense is vital to the perception of a "future" that is in any way different from a "present." Stories construct beginnings and endings; they impose beginnings and endings on the flow of experience. We perform these stories into lived experience and meaning.

STRUCTURALISM   Structuralists look at the foundational structures implicit in all productions of a culture and undertake an analysis of the many parts that create something to get a better understanding of the creation. The basic premise of structuralism is that all things have a structure below the level of meaning, and that this structure constitutes the reality of that thing. The vast majority of psychological practices are based in structuralism.

SUBJECT   The subject is an entity that is self-aware and capable of choosing how to act. Foucault was consistently opposed to 19th-century and phenomenological notions of a universal and timeless subject that was at the source of how one made sense of the world and that was the foundation of all thought and action. The problem with this conception of the subject, according to Foucault and other thinkers in the 1960s, was that it fixed the status quo and attached people to specific identities that could never be changed.

TEXT ANALOGY   The text analogy proposes that meaning is derived from the storying of our experience. It is the stories that persons tell that determine meaning about their lives.

TOTALIZATION TECHNIQUES   Totalization techniques are culturally produced notions about the specification of personhood.

UNIQUE OUTCOMES   Unique outcomes provide a starting point for re-authoring conversations. They make available a point of entry into the alternative story lines of people's lives that, at the outset of these conversations, become visible as thin traces, which are full of gaps and not clearly named. As these conversations proceed, therapists build a scaffold through questions that encourage people to fill these gaps. Through a telling of a re-authored story, people are able to identify previously neglected but vital aspects of lived experiences—aspects that could not have been predicted from a reading of the dominant problem story.

UNIVERSAL CATEGORIES   Narrative therapy is firmly and consistently opposed to the notion of universal categories and essences, "things" that existed in unchanged form in all times and places, such as the state, madness, sexuality, criminality, and so on. These things only acquire a real (and changing) existence as the result of specific historical activities and reflection.

VANCOUVER SCHOOL FOR NARRATIVE THERAPY   Established in 1992 by Stephen Madigan as the first narrative therapy training site in the northern hemisphere. The school offers certificate training programs in narrative therapy (http://www.therapeuticconversations.com)

# Suggested Readings

Bateson, G. (1972). *Steps to an ecology of mind: Collected essays in anthropology, psychiatry, evolution, and epistemology.* Chicago, IL: University of Chicago Press.

Bateson, G. (1979). *Mind and nature: A necessary unity.* New York, NY: Dutton.

Bakhtin, M. M. (1986). *Speech genres and other late essays* (V. McGee, Trans.). Austin: University of Texas Press.

Bird, J. (2004). *Talk the sings.* Auckland, New Zealand: Edge Press.

Breggin, P. (1994). *Toxic psychiatry: Why therapy, empathy, and love must replace the drugs, electroshock, and biochemical theories of the new psychiatry.* New York, NY: St. Martin's Press.

Bruner, J. (1990). *Acts of meaning.* Cambridge, MA: Harvard University Press.

Caplan, P. J. (1995). *They say you're crazy: How the world's most powerful psychiatrists decide who's normal.* Reading, MA: Addison Wesley.

Epston, D. (1988). *Collected papers.* Adelaide, South Australia: Dulwich Centre Publications.

Epston, D. (1998). *Catching up with David Epston: A collection of narrative practice-based papers, 1991–1996—by David Epston.* Adelaide, South Australia: Dulwich Centre Publications.

Foucault, M. (1965). *Madness and civilization: A history of insanity in the age of reason.* New York, NY: Random House.

Foucault, M. (1979). *Discipline and punish: The birth of the prison.* Middlesex, England: Peregrine Books.

Foucault, M. (1980). *Power/Knowledge: Selected interviews and writings.* New York, NY: Pantheon Books.

Foucault, M. (1989). *Foucault live: Collected interviews, 1961–1984* (S. Lotringer, Ed.). New York, NY: Semiotext(e).

Geertz, C. (1973). *The interpretation of cultures.* New York, NY: Basic Books.

Madigan, S. (1991). Discursive restraints in therapist practice: Situating therapist questions in the presence of the family—a new model for supervision. *International Journal of Narrative Therapy and Community Work, 3,* 13–21.

Madigan, S. (1992). The application of Michel Foucault's philosophy in the problem externalizing discourse of Michael White. *British Journal of Family Therapy, 14,* 265–279.

Madigan, S. (1996). The politics of identity: Considering the socio-political and cultural context in the externalizing of internalized problem conversations [Special edition on narrative ideas]. *Journal of Systemic Therapies, 15,* 47–63.

Madigan, S. (1997). Re-remembering lost identities: Narrative therapy with children and adolescents. In D. Nylund & C. Smith (Eds.), *Narrative therapies with children and adolescents* (pp. 338–355). New York, NY: Guilford Press.

Madigan, S. (1999). Destabilizing chronic identities of depression and retirement. In I. Parker (Ed.), *Deconstructing psychotherapy* (pp. 150–163). Thousand Oaks, CA: Sage.

Madigan, S. (2003). Injurious speech: Counter-viewing eight conversational habits of highly effective problems. *International Journal of Narrative Therapy and Community Work, 2,* 12–19.

Madigan, S. (2007). Watchers of the watched: Self-surveillance in everyday life. In C. Brown & T. Augusta-Scott (Eds.), *Postmodernism and narrative therapy* (pp. 67–78). Thousand Oaks, CA: Sage.

Madigan, S. (2008). Anticipating hope within conversational domains of despair. In I. McCarthy & J. Sheehan (Eds.), *Hope and despair* (pp. 104–112). London, England: Bruner Mazel.

Madigan, S., & Epston, D. (1995). From "spy-chiatric gaze" to communities of concern: From professional monologue to dialogue. In S. Friedman (Ed.), *The reflecting team in action: Innovations in clinical practice* (pp. 257–276). New York, NY: Guilford Press.

Madigan, S., & Goldner, E. (1998). A narrative approach to anorexia: Reflexivity, discourse, and questions. In M. Hoyt (Ed.), *The handbook of constructive therapies* (pp. 96–107). San Francisco, CA: Jossey Bass.

Madigan, S., & Law, I. (1998). *PRAXIS: Situating discourse, feminism, and politics in narrative therapies.* Vancouver, British Columbia, Canada: Yaletown Family Therapy Press.

Sampson, E. (1993). *Celebrating the other: A dialogic account of human nature.* San Francisco, CA: Westview Press.

Shotter, J., & Gergen, K. (1989). *Texts of identity.* Newbury Park, CA: Sage.

White, M. (1995). *Re-authoring lives: Interviews and essays.* Adelaide, South Australia: Dulwich Centre Publications.

White, M., & Epston, D. (1990). *Narrative means to therapeutic ends.* New York, NY: Norton.

# References

Akinyela, M. (2005, May). *Oral cultures and the use of metaphors in the therapeutic conversations.* Keynote speech at the Therapeutic Conversations Conference, Vancouver, British Columbia, Canada.

Andersen, T. (1987). The reflecting team: Dialogue and meta-dialogue in clinical work. *Family Process, 26,* 415–428. doi:10.1111/j.1545-5300.1987.00415.x

Anderson, W. (1990). *Reality isn't what it used to be.* San Francisco, CA: Harper & Row.

Armstrong, T. (1989). *Michel Foucault, philosopher.* New York, NY: Routledge.

Augusta-Scott, T. (2007). Conversations with men about women's violence: Ending men's violence by challenging gender essentialism. In T. Augusta-Scott & C. Brown (Eds.), *Narrative therapy: Making meaning, making lives* (pp. 197–210). New York, NY: Sage.

Bakhtin, M. M. (1981). *The dialogic imagination.* Austin, TX: University of Texas Press.

Bakhtin, M. M. (1986). *Speech genres and other late essays* (V. McGee, Trans.). Austin, TX: University of Texas Press.

Bateson, G. (1972). *Steps to an ecology of mind: Collected essays in anthropology, psychiatry, evolution, and epistemology.* Chicago, IL: University of Chicago Press.

Bateson, G. (1979). *Mind and nature: A necessary unity.* New York, NY: Dutton.

Besa, D. (1994). Evaluating narrative family therapy using single-system research designs. *Research on Social Work Practice, 4,* 309–325.

Billig, M. (1990). Collective memory, ideology and the British Royal Family. In D. Middleton & D. Edwards (Eds.), *Collective remembering* (pp. 13–31). London, England: Sage.

Bird, J. (2000). *Talk hearts narrative.* Auckland, New Zealand: Edge Press.

Bird, J. (2004). *Talk the sings.* Auckland, New Zealand: Edge Press.

Borden, A. (2007). Every conversation is an opportunity: Negotiating identity in group settings. *The International Journal of Narrative Therapy and Community Work, 4*, 38–53.

Bordo, S. (1989). The body and the reproduction of femininity: A feminist appropriation of Foucault. In A. M. Jaggar & S. R. Bordo (Eds.), *Feminist reconstructions of being and knowing* (pp. 13–33). New Brunswick, NJ: Rutgers University Press.

Bordo, S. (1993). *Unbearable weight.* Berkeley: University of California Press.

Breggin, P. (1994). *Toxic psychiatry: Why therapy, empathy, and love must replace the drugs, electroshock, and biochemical theories of the new psychiatry.* New York, NY: St. Martin's Press.

Breggin, P., & Breggin, G. R. (1994). *Talking back to Prozac: What doctors won't tell you about today's most controversial drug.* New York, NY: St. Martin's Press.

Breggin, P., & Breggin, G. R. (1997). *War against children of color: Psychiatry targets inner-city youth.* Monroe, ME: Common Courage Press.

Bruner, E. M. (1986). Ethnography as narrative. In V. W. Turner & E. M. Bruner (Eds.), *The anthropology of experience* (pp. 139–157). Chicago: University of Illinois Press.

Bruner, J. (1986). *Actual minds, possible worlds.* Cambridge, MA: Harvard University Press.

Bruner, J. (1990). *Acts of meaning.* Cambridge, MA: Harvard University Press.

Bruner, J. (1991). The narrative construction of reality. *Critical Inquiry, 18,* 1–21.

Bruyn, S. (1990). *The human perspective: The methodology of participant observation.* Englewood Cliff, NJ: Prentice Hall.

Butler, J. (1997). *Excitable speech: A politics of the performance.* New York, NY: Routledge.

Caplan, P. J. (1984). The myth of women's masochism. *American Psychologist, 39,* 130–139. doi:10.1037/0003-066X.39.2.130

Caplan, P. J. (1991). Delusional dominating personality disorder (PDPD). *Feminism & Psychology, 1,* 171–174. doi:10.1177/0959353591011020

Caplan, P. J. (1994). *You're smarter than they make you feel: How the experts intimidate us and what we can do about it.* New York, NY: Free Press.

Caplan, P. J. (1995). *They say you're crazy: How the world's most powerful psychiatrists decide who's normal.* Reading, MA: Addison Wesley.

Caplan, P. J., & Cosgrove, L. (Eds.). (2004). *Bias in psychiatric diagnosis.* New York, NY: Jason Aronson.

Carlson, J., & Kjos, D. (1999). *Narrative therapy with Stephen Madigan* [Family Therapy with the Expert Series Videotape]. Boston, MA: Allyn and Bacon.

Clark, K., & Holquist, M. (1984). *Mikhail Bakhtin.* Cambridge, MA: Harvard University Press.

Crapanzano, V. (1990). On self characterization. In S. Stigler, R.A. Shweder, & G. S. Herdt (Eds.), *Cutural psychology: Essays on comparative human development* (pp. 401–425). Cambridge, England: Cambridge University Press.

Crowe, M. (2000). Constructing normality: A discourse analysis of the *DSM–IV*. *Journal of Psychiatric and Mental Health Nursing, 7*, 69–77. doi:10.1046/j.1365-2850.2000.00261.x

Daniels, H., Cole, M., & Wertsch, J. (Eds.). (2007). *The Cambridge companion to Vygotsky*. New York, NY: Cambridge University Press.

Davies, B., & Harre, R. (1990). Positioning: Conversation and the production of selves. *Journal for the Theory of Social Behaviour, 20*, 43–63. doi:10.1111/j.1468-5914.1990.tb00174.x

Denborough, D. (2008). *Collective narrative practice: Responding to individuals, groups, and communities who have experienced trauma*. Adelaide, South Australia: Dulwich Centre Publications.

Denborough, D., Koolmatrie, C., Mununggirritj, D., Marika, D., Dhurrkay, W., & Yunupingu, M. (2006). Linking stories and initiatives: A narrative approach to working with the skills and knowledge of communities. *The International Journal of Narrative Therapy and Community Work, 2*, 19–51.

Derrida, J. (1991). *A Derrida reader: Between the blinds* (P. Kamuf, Ed.). New York, NY: Columbia University Press.

Diamond, I., & Quinby, L. (1988). *Feminism and Foucault: Reflections on resistance*. Boston, MA: Northeastern University Press.

Dickerson, V. C. (2004). Young women struggling for an identity. *Family Process, 43*, 337–348. doi:10.1111/j.1545-5300.2004.00026.x

Dickerson, V. C. (2009). Remembering the future: Situating oneself in a constantly evolving field. *Journal of Systemic Therapies, 26*, 23–37.

Dickerson, V. C. (in press). Allies against self-doubt. *Journal of Brief Therapy*.

Dickerson, V. C., & Zimmerman, J. (1992). Families and adolescents: Escaping problem lifestyles. *Family Process, 31*, 341–353. doi:10.1111/j.1545-5300.1992.00341.x

Dickerson, V. C., & Zimmerman, J. (1996). *If problems talked: Narrative therapy in action*. New York, NY: Guilford Press.

Dreyfus, H., & Rabinow, P. (1983). *Michel Foucault: Beyond structuralism and hermeneutics* (2nd ed.). Chicago, IL: University of Chicago Press.

Eagleton, T. (1991). *An introduction to ideology*. New York, NY: Verso.

Epston, D. (1986). Nightwatching: An approach to night fears. *Dulwich Centre Review*, 28–39.

Epston, D. (1988). *Collected papers*. Adelaide, South Australia: Dulwich Centre Publications.

Epston, D. (1994). The problem with originality. *Dulwich Centre Newsletter, 4*.

Epston, D. (1998). *Catching up with David Epston: A collection of narrative practice-based papers, 1991–1996.* Adelaide, South Australia: Dulwich Centre Publications.

Epston, D. (2009). *Catching up with David Epston: Down under and up over.* Warrington, England: AFT.

Epston, D., & Roth, S. (1995). In S. Friedman (Ed.), *The reflecting team in action: Collaborative practice in family therapy* (pp. 39–46). New York, NY: Guilford Press.

Epston, D., & White, M. (1990). Consulting your consultants: The documentation of alternative knowledges. *Dulwich Centre Newsletter, 4,* 25–35.

Epston, D., & White, M. (1992). *Experience, contradiction, narrative and imagination: Selected papers of David Epston and Michael White, 1989–1991.* Adelaide, South Australia: Dulwich Centre Publications.

Espin, O. M. (1995). On knowing you are the unknown: Women of color constructing psychology. In J. Adleman & G. Enguidanos (Eds.), *Racism in the lives of women: Testimony, theory, and guides to antiracist practice* (pp. 127–136). New York, NY: Haworth Press.

Fish, S. (1980). *Is there a text in this class? The authority of interpretive communities.* Cambridge, MA: Harvard University Press.

Foucault, M. (1965). *Madness and civilization: A history of insanity in the age of reason.* New York, NY: Random House.

Foucault, M. (1972). *The archaeology of knowledge and the discourse on language* (A. M. Sheridan Smith, Trans.). New York, NY: Pantheon.

Foucault, M. (1973). *The birth of the clinic: An archeology of medical perception.* London, England: Tavistock.

Foucault, M. (1977). Nietzsche, genealogy, history. In D. F. Bouchard (Ed.), *Language counter-memory, practice: Selected essays and interviews* (pp. 139–164). Ithaca, NY: Cornell University Press.

Foucault, M. (1979). *Discipline and punish: The birth of the prison.* Middlesex, England: Peregrine Books.

Foucault, M. (1980). *Power/knowledge: Selected interviews and writings.* New York, NY: Pantheon Books.

Foucault, M. (1983). The subject and power. In H. Dreyfus & P. Rabinow (Eds.), *Michel Foucault: Beyond structuralism and hermeneutics* (2nd ed., pp. 208–228). Chicago, IL: University of Chicago Press.

Foucault, M. (1984a). *The history of sexuality.* Middlesex, England: Peregrine Books.

Foucault, M. (1984b). Space, knowledge and power. In P. Rabinow (Ed.), *The Foucault reader* (pp. 239–256). New York, NY: Pantheon Books.

Foucault, M. (1989). *Foucault live: Collected interviews, 1961–1984* (S. Lotringer, Ed.). New York, NY: Semiotext(e).

Foucault, M. (1994a). The ethics of the concern for self as a practice of freedom. In P. Rabinow (Ed.), *Ethics: Subjectivity and truth: Vol. 1. Essential works of Foucault 1954–1984* (pp. 281–302). London, England: Penguin Press.

Foucault, M. (1994b). On the genealogy of ethics: An overview of work in progress. In P. Rabinow (Ed.), *Ethics: Subjectivity and truth: Vol. 1. Essential works of Foucault 1954–1984* (pp. 253–280). London, England: Penguin Press.

Foucault, M. (1997). *The politics of truth* (S. Lotringer, Ed.). New York, NY: Semiotext(e).

Freedman, J., & Combs, G. (1996). *Narrative therapy: The social construction of preferred realities.* New York, NY: Norton.

Freedman, J., & Combs, G. (2002). *Narrative therapy with couples—and a whole lot more.* Adelaide, South Australia: Dulwich Centre Publications.

Freeman, J., Epston, D., & Lobivits, D. (1997). *Playful approaches to serious problems.* New York, NY: Norton.

Geertz, C. (1973). *The interpretation of cultures.* New York, NY: Basic Books.

Geertz, C. (1976). From nature's point of view: On the nature of anthropological understanding. In K. H. Basso & H. A. Selby (Eds.), *Meaning in anthropology* (pp. 89–95). Albuquerque: University of New Mexico Press.

Geertz, C. (1983). *Local knowledge: Further essays in interpretive anthropology.* New York, NY: Basic Books.

Geertz, C. (1988). *Works and lives: The anthropologist as author.* Stanford, CA: Stanford University Press.

Gergen, K. (1989). Warranting voice and the elaboration of self. In J. Shotter & K. Gergen (Eds.), *Texts of identity* (pp. 56–68). London, England: Sage.

Gergen, K. (1991). *The saturated self: Dilemmas of identity in contemporary life.* New York, NY: Basic Books.

Gergen, K. (2009). *Relational being: Beyond self and community.* Oxford, England: Oxford University Press.

Gergen, M. M., & Gergen, K. J. (1984). The social construction of narrative accounts. In K. J. Gergen & M. M. Gergen (Eds.), *Historical social psychology* (pp. 102–107). Hillsdale, NY: Erlbaum.

Goffman, E. (1961). *Asylums: Essays in the social situation of mental patients and other inmates.* New York, NY: Doubleday.

Goldstein, J. (1981). *Michel Foucault: Remarks on Marx.* New York, NY: Semiotext(e).

Gollan, S., & White, M. (1995, March). *The Aboriginal project.* Paper presented at the Family Networker conference, Washington, DC.

Gremillion, H. (2003). *Feeding anorexia: Gender and power at a treatment center.* Durham, NC: Duke University Press.

Grieves, L. (1998). From beginning to start: The Vancouver Anti-Anorexia/ Anti-Bulimia League. In S. Madigan & I. Law (Eds.), *PRAXIS: Situating discourse, feminism and politics in narrative therapies* (pp. 195–206). Vancouver, British Columbia, Canada: Yaletown Family Therapy Press.

Gutting, G. (Ed.). (1994). *The Cambridge companion to Foucault.* Cambridge, England: Cambridge University Press.

Hall, R., Mclean, C., & White, C. (1994). Special edition on accountability. *Dulwich Centre Newsletter, 2,* 79.

Hardy, K. (2004, May). *Boys in the hood.* Keynote speech at the Therapeutic Conversations Conference, Vancouver, British Columbia, Canada.

Hare-Mustin, R., & Maracek, J. (1995). Feminism and postmodernism: Dilemmas and points of resistance. *Dulwich Centre Newsletter, 4,* 13–19.

Harstock, S. (1990). Foucault on power: A theory for women? In L. Nicholson (Ed.), *Feminism/postmodernism* (pp. 157–175). New York, NY: Routledge.

Hedtke, L., & Winslade, J. (2004/2005). The use of the subjunctive in remembering conversations with those who are grieving. *OMEGA, 50,* 197–215.

Hoagwood, K. (1993). Poststructuralist histoticism and the psychological construction of anxiety disorders. *The Journal of Psychology, 127,* 105–122.

Horkheimer, M., & Adorno, T. (1972). *Dialectic of enlightenment* (J. Cumming, Trans.). New York, NY: Herder & Herder.

Huyssen, A. (1990). Mapping the postmodern. In L. Nicholson (Ed.), *Feminism/ postmodernism* (pp. 234–279). New York, NY: Routledge.

Jameson, F. (1991). *Postmodernism or the cultural logic of late capitalism.* Durham, NC: Duke University Press.

Jenkins, A. (1990). *Invitations to responsibility: The therapeutic engagement with men who are violent and abusive.* Adelaide, South Australia: Dulwich Centre Publications.

Jenkins, A. (2009). *Becoming ethical: A parallel political journey with men who have abused.* Dorset, England: Russell House.

Justice, B., & Justice, R. (1979). Incest in a family/group survivial pattern. *Archives of General Psychiatry, 14,* 31–40.

Kamsler, A. (1990). *Her-story in the making: Therapy with women who were sexually abused in childhood.* Adelaide, South Australia: Dulwich Centre Publications.

Kearney, R., & Rainwater, M. (1996). *The continental philosophy reader.* New York, NY: Routledge.

Keeney, B. (1983). *Aesthetics of change.* New York, NY: Guilford Press.

Law, I., & Madigan, S. (Eds.). (1994). Power and politics in practice [Special issue]. *Dulwich Centre Newsletter, 1.*

Liapunov, V., & Holquist, M. (1993). *M. M. Bakhtin: Toward a philosophy of the act.* Austin, TX: University of Texas Press.

Madigan, S. (1991a). Discursive restraints in therapist practice: Situating therapist questions in the presence of the family—a new model for supervision (Cheryl White, Ed.). *International Journal of Narrative Therapy and Community Work, 3*, 13–21.

Madigan, S. (1991b). A public place for schizophrenia: An interview with C. Christian Beels. *International Journal of Narrative Therapy and Community Work, 2*, 9–11.

Madigan, S. (1992). The application of Michel Foucault's philosophy in the problem externalizing discourse of Michael White [Additional commentary by Deborah Anne Luepnitz, rejoinder by S. Madigan]. *Journal of Family Therapy, 14*, 265–279.

Madigan, S. (1993a). Questions about questions: Situating the therapist's curiosity in front of the family. In S. Gilligan & R. Price (Eds.), *Therapeutic conversations* (pp. 219–230). New York, NY: Norton.

Madigan, S. (1993b). Rituals about rituals: A commentary on "Therapeutic rituals: Passages into new identities" by S. Gilligan. In S. Gilligan & R. Price (Eds.), *Therapeutic conversations* (253–257). New York, NY: Norton.

Madigan, S. (1994). The discourse unnoticed: Story-telling rights and the deconstruction of longstanding problems. *Journal of Child and Youth Care, 9*, 79–86.

Madigan, S. (1996). The politics of identity: Considering the socio-political and cultural context in the externalizing of internalized problem conversations [Special edition on narrative ideas]. *Journal of Systemic Therapies, 15*, 47–63.

Madigan, S. (1997). Re-considering memory: Re-remembering lost identities back toward re-membered selves. In C. Smith & D. Nylund (Eds.), *Narrative therapies with children and adolescents* (pp. 338–355). New York, NY: Guilford Press.

Madigan, S. (1999). Destabilizing chronic identities of depression and retirement. In I. Parker (Ed.), *Deconstructing psychotherapy* (pp. 56–67). London, England: Sage.

Madigan, S. (2003). Injurious speech: Counter-viewing eight conversational habits of highly effective problems. *International Journal of Narrative Therapy and Community Work, 2*, 12–19.

Madigan, S. (2004). Re-writing Tom: Undermining descriptions of chronicity through therapeutic letter writing campaigns. In J. Carlson (Ed.), *My finest hour: Family therapy with the experts* (pp. 65–74). Boston, MA: Allyn and Bacon.

Madigan, S. (2007). Watchers of the watched—self-surveillance in everyday life. In C. Brown & T. Augusta-Scott (Eds.), *Postmodernism and narrative therapy* (pp. 67–78). New York, NY: Sage.

Madigan, S. (2008). Anticipating hope within conversational domains of despair. In I. McCarthy & J. Sheehan (Eds.), *Hope and despair* (pp. 104–112). London, England: Bruner Mazel.

Madigan, S. (2009). Therapy as community connections. In J. Kottler & J. Carlson (Eds.), *Creative breakthroughs in therapy: Tales of transformation and astonishment* (pp. 65–80). New York, NY: Wiley.

Madigan S., & Epston, D. (1995). From "spy-chiatric gaze" to communities of concern: From professional monologue to dialogue. In S. Friedman (Ed.), *The reflecting team in action: Collaborative practice in family therapy* (257–276). New York, NY: Guilford Press.

Madigan, S., & Goldner, E. (1998). A narrative approach to anorexia: Reflexivity, discourse and questions. In M. Hoyt (Ed.), *The handbook of constructive therapies* (pp. 96–107). San Francisco, CA: Jossey-Bass.

Madigan, S., & Law, I. (1992). Discourse not language: The shift from a modernist view of language to the post-modern analysis of discourse in family therapy (Cheryl White, Ed.). *International Journal of Narrative Therapy and Community Work, 1.*

Madigan, S., & Law, I. (Eds.). (1998). *PRAXIS: Situating discourse, feminism and politics in narrative therapies.* Vancouver, British Columbia, Canada: Yaletown Family Therapy Press.

Madison, D. (2005). *Critical ethnography.* New York, NY: Sage.

Madsen, W. (2007). *Collaborative therapy with multi-stressed families.* New York, NY: Norton.

Maisel, R., Epston, D., & Borden, A. (2004). *Biting the hand that starves you: Inspiring resistance in anorexia/bulimia.* New York, NY: Norton.

McHoul, A., & Grace, W. (1993). *A Foucault primer: Discourse, power and the subject.* New York, NY: New York University Press.

McLeod, J. (1997). *Narrative and psychotherapy.* London, England: Sage.

McLeod, J. (2004). The significance of narrative and storytelling in postpsychological counseling and psychotherapy. In A. Lieblich, D. P. McAdams, & R. Josselson (Eds.), *Healing plots: The narrative basis for psychotherapy* (11–27). Washington, DC: American Psychological Association.

Miller, J. (1993). *The passion of Michel Foucault.* New York, NY: Anchor Books.

Moules, N. (2003). Therapy on paper: Therapeutic letters and the tone of relationship. *Journal of Systemic Therapies, 22,* 33–49.

Moules, N. (2007). *Hermeneutic inquiry: Paying heed to history and Hermes. An ancestral, substantive, and methodological tale.* Unpublished manuscript.

Munro, C. (1987). White and the cybernetic therapies: News of difference. *The Australian and New Zealand Journal of Family Therapy, 8,* 183–192.

Myerhoff, B. (1982). Life history among the elderly: Performance, visibility and re-membering. In J. Ruby (Ed.), *A crack in the mirror: Reflexive perspectives in anthropology* (pp. 99–117). Philadelphia: University of Pennsylvania Press.

Myerhoff, B. (1986). "Life not death in Venice": Its second life. In V. W. Turner & E. M. Bruner (Eds.), *The anthropology of experience* (pp. 73–81). Chicago: University of Illinois Press.

Myerhoff, B. (1992). *Remembered lives: The work of ritual, storytelling, and growing older* (M. Kaminsky, Ed.). Ann Arbor: University of Michigan Press.

Nylund, D. (2000). *Treating Huckleberry Finn: A new narrative approach with kids diagnosed ADD/ADHD.* San Francisco, CA: Jossey-Bass.

Nylund, D. (2002a). Poetic means to anti-anorexic ends. *Journal of Systemic Therapies, 21*(4), 18–34. doi:10.1521/jsyt.21.4.18.23323

Nylund, D. (2002b). Understanding and coping with ADD/ADHD. In J. Biederman & L. Biederman (Eds.), *Parent school: Simple lessons from the leading experts on being a mom and dad* (pp. 291–296). New York, NY: M. Evans.

Nylund, D. (2003). Narrative therapy as a counter-hegemonic practice. *Men and Masculinities, 5,* 386–394. doi:10.1177/1097184X03251086

Nylund, D. (2004a). Deconstructing masculinity through popular culture texts. *Narrative Network News, 27,* 35–39.

Nylund, D. (2004b). The mass media and masculinity: Working with men who have been violent. In S. Madigan (Ed.), *Therapeutic conversations 5: Therapy from the outside in* (pp. 177–191). Vancouver, British Columbia, Canada: Yaletown Family Therapy Press.

Nylund, D. (2004c). When in Rome: Homophobia, heterosexism, and sports talk radio. *Journal of Sport and Social Issues, 28,* 136–168. doi:10.1177/0193723504264409

Nylund, D. (2006a). Critical multiculturalism, whiteness, and social work: Towards a more radical view of cultural competence. *Journal of Progressive Human Services, 17*(2), 27–42. doi:10.1300/J059v17n02_03

Nylund, D. (2006b). Deconstructing patriarchy and masculinity with teen fathers: A narrative approach. In R. Evans, H. S. Holgate, & F. K. O. Yuen (Eds.), *Teenage pregnancy and parenthood* (pp. 157–167). New York, NY: Routledge.

Nylund, D. (2007a). *Beer, babes, and balls: Masculinity and sports talk radio.* Albany, NY: SUNY Press.

Nylund, D. (2007b). Reading Harry Potter: Popular culture, queer theory, and the fashioning of youth identity. *Journal of Systemic Therapies, 26*(2), 13–24. doi:10.1521/jsyt.2007.26.2.13

Nylund, D., & Ceske, K. (1997). Voices of political resistance: Young women's co-research in anti-depression. In C. Smith & D. Nylund (Eds.), *Narrative therapies with children and adolescents* (pp. 356–381). New York, NY: Guilford Press.

Nylund, D., & Corsiglia, V. (1993). Internalized other questioning with men who are violent. *Dulwich Centre Newsletter, 2,* 29–34.

Nylund, D., & Corsiglia, V. (1994). Attention to the deficits in attention deficit disorder: Deconstructing the diagnosis and bringing forth children's special abilities. *Journal of Collaborative Therapies, 2*(2), 7–16.

Nylund, D., & Corsiglia, V. (1996). From deficits to special abilities: Working narratively with children labeled ADHD. In M. Hoyt (Ed.), *Constructive therapies 2* (pp. 163–183). New York, NY: Guilford Press.

Nylund, D., & Hoyt, M. (1997). The joy of narrative: An exercise for learning from our internalized clients. *Journal of Systemic Therapies, 16,* 361–366.

Nylund, D., & Thomas, J. (1997). Situating therapist's questions in the presence of the family: A qualitative inquiry. *Journal of Systemic Therapies, 16,* 211–228.

Nylund, D., Tilsen, J., & Grieves, L. (2007). The gender binary: Theory and lived experience. *International Journal of Narrative Therapy and Community Work, 3,* 46–53.

O'Farrell, C. (2005). *Michel Foucault.* London, England: Sage.

Parker, I. (1989). Discourse and power. In J. Shotter & K. Gergen (Eds.), *Texts of identity* (pp. 16–25). London, England: Sage.

Parker, I. (1998). *Social construction, discourse and realism.* London, England: Sage.

Parker, I. (2008). *Being human: Reflections on mental distress in society* (I. A. Morgan, Ed.). Ross-on-Wye, England: PCCS Books.

Prado, G. (1995). *Starting with Foucault: An introduction to genealogy.* Boulder, CO: Westview Press.

Reynolds, V. (2008). An ethic of resistance: Frontline worker as activist. *Women Making Waves, 19,* 12–14.

Reynolds, V. (2010). Doing justice: A witnessing stance in therapeutic work alongside survivors of torture and political violence. In J. Raskin, S. Bridges, & R. Neimeyer (Eds.), *Studies in meaning 4: Constuctivist perspectives on theory, practice, and social justice.* New York, NY: Pace University Press.

Ricoeur, P. (1984). *Time and narrative* (Vol. 1). Chicago, IL: The University of Chicago Press.

Rorty, R. (1979). *Philosophy and the mirror of nature.* Princeton, NY: Princeton University Press.

Rose, N. (1989). Individualizing psychology. In J. Shotter & K. Gergen (Eds.), *Texts of identity* (pp. 64–72). London, England: Sage.

Rosen, S. (1987). *Hermeneutics as politics.* New York, NY: Oxford University Press.

Said, E. (2003). *Freud and the non-European.* New York, NY: Verso.

Sampson, E. (1989). The deconstruction of the self. In J. Shotter & K. Gergen (Eds.), *Texts of identity* (pp. 3–11). Newbury Park, CA: Sage.

Sampson, E. (1993). *Celebrating the other: A dialogic account of human nature*. San Francisco, CA: Westview Press.

Sanders, C. (1997). Re-authoring problem identities: Small victories with young persons captured by substance misuse. In C. Smith & D. Nylund (Eds.), *Narrative therapies with children and adolescents* (pp. 400–422). New York, NY: Guilford Press.

Sanders, C. (1998). Substance misuse dilemmas: A postmodern inquiry. In S. Madigan & I. Law (Eds.), *PRAXIS: Situating discourse, feminism, and politics in narrative therapies* (pp. 141–162). Vancouver, British Columbia, Canada: Yaletown Family Therapy Press.

Sanders, C. (2007). A poetics of resistance: Compassionate practice in substance misuse therapy. In C. Brown & T. Augusta-Scott (Eds.), *Narrative therapy: Making meaning, making lives* (pp. 59–76). Thousand Oaks, CA: Sage.

Sanders, C., & Thomson, G. (1994). Opening space: Towards dialogue and discovery. *Journal of Child and Youth Care, 9*(2), 1–11.

Seymour, F., & Epston, D. (1989). Childhood stealing. *The Australian and New Zealand Journal of Family Therapy, 10,* 137–143.

Shotter, J. (1989). Social accountability and the social construction of "you." In J. Shotter & K. Gergen (Eds.), *Texts of identity* (pp. 4–14). London, England: Sage.

Shotter, J. (1990a). *The social construction of remembering and forgetting*. In D. Middleton & D. Edwards (Eds.), *Collective remembering* (pp. 120–138). London, England: Sage.

Shotter, J. (1990b). Social individuality versus possessive individualism: The sounds of silence. In I. Parker & J. Shotter (Eds.), *Deconstructing social psychology* (pp. 153–160). London, England: Routledge.

Shotter, J., & Gergen, K. (1989). *Texts of identity*. Newbury Park, CA: Sage.

Simons, J. (1995). *Foucault and the political*. New York, NY: Routledge.

Smith, C., & Nylund, D. (Eds.). (1997). *Narrative therapies with children and adolescents*. New York, NY: Guilford Press.

Speedy, J. (2004). Living a more peopled life: Definitional ceremony as inquiry into psychotherapy "outcomes." *International Journal of Narrative Therapy and Community Work, 3,* 43–53.

Spivak, G. (1996). Diaspora old and new: Women in the transnational world. *Textual Practice, 10,* 245–269.

Szasz, T. (2001). *Pharmacracy medicine and politics in America*. Westport, CT: Praeger.

Tamasese, K., & Waldegrave, C. (1990). Social justice. *Dulwich Centre Newsletter, 1.*

Taylor, C. (1989). *Sources of the self.* Cambridge, MA: Harvard University Press.

Tilsen, J., & Nylund, D. (2008). Psychotherapy research, the recovery movement, and practice-based evidence. *The Journal of Social Work in Disability & Rehabilitation, 7,* 340–354.

Tilsen, J., & Nylund, D. (2009). Popular culture texts and young people: Making meaning, honoring resistance, and becoming Harry Potter. *International Journal of Narrative Therapy and Community Work, 1,* 16–19.

Tinker, D. E., & Ramer, J. C. (1983). Anorexia nervosa: Staff subversion of therapy. *Journal of Adolescent Health Care, 4,* 35–39. doi:10.1016/S0197-0070(83)80226-5

Tomm, K. (1984a). One perspective on the Milan Systemic Approach: Part I. Overview of development, theory and practice. *Journal of Marital and Family Therapy, 10,* 113–125. doi:10.1111/j.1752-0606.1984.tb00001.x

Tomm, K. (1984b). One perspective on the Milan Systemic Approach: Part II. Description of session format, interviewing style and interventions. *Journal of Marital and Family Therapy, 10,* 253–271. doi:10.1111/j.1752-0606.1984.tb00016.x

Tomm, K. (1986). On incorporating the therapist in a scientific theory of family therapy. *Journal of Marital and Family Therapy, 12,* 373–378. doi:10.1111/j.1752-0606.1986.tb00669.x

Tomm, K. (1987a). Interventive interviewing: Part I. Strategizing as a fourth guideline for the therapist. *Family Process, 26,* 3–13. doi:10.1111/j.1545-5300.1987.00003.x

Tomm, K. (1987b). Interventive interviewing: Part II. Reflexive questioning as a means to enable self-healing. *Family Process, 26,* 167–183. doi:10.1111/j.1545-5300.1987.00167.x

Tomm, K. (1988). Interventive interviewing: Part III. Intending to ask lineal, circular, reflexive or strategic questions? *Family Process, 27,* 1–15. doi:10.1111/j.1545-5300.1988.00001.x

Tomm, K. (1989). Externalizing problems and internalizing personal agency. *Journal of Strategic & Systemic Therapies, 8,* 16–22.

Turner, V. (1969). *The ritual process.* Ithaca, NY: Cornell University Press.

Turner, V. (1974). *Drama, fields and metaphor.* Ithaca, NY: Cornell University Press.

Turner, V. (1980). Social dramas and stories about them. *Critical Inquiry, 7,* 141–168.

Turner, V. (1981). Social dramas and stories about them. In W. J. T. Mitchell (Ed.), *On narrative* (pp. 137–164). Chicago, IL: University of Chicago Press.

Turner, V. (1986). *The anthropology of performance.* New York, NY: PAJ.

Tyler, S. (1986). *The unspeakable: Discourse, dialogue and rhetoric in the postmodern world.* Madison: University of Wisconsin Press.

Tyler, S. A. (1990). Eye of newt, toe of frog: Post-modernism and the context of theory in family therapy. In P. Keeney, B. B. Nolan, & W. Madsen (Eds.), *The systemic therapist.* St. Paul, MN: Systemic Therapy Press.

Vancouver Anti-Anorexia/Bulimia League. (1998). Editorial. *Revive Magazine.* Vancouver, British Columbia, Canada: Yaletown Family Therapy Publications.

Vromans, L. (2008). *Process and outcome of narrative therapy for major depressive disorder in adults: Narrative reflexivity, working alliance, and improved symptom and inter-personal outcomes.* Unpublished doctoral dissertation, Queensland University of Technology, Australia.

Vygotsky, L. S. (1978). *Mind in society.* Cambridge, MA: Harvard University Press.

Wade, A. (1996). Resistance knowledges: Therapy with aboriginal persons who have experienced violence. In P. H. Stephenson, S. J. Elliott, L. T. Foster, & J. Harris (Eds.), *A persistent spirit: Towards understanding aboriginal health in British Columbia* (pp. 167–206). Vancouver, British Columbia, Canada: University of British Columbia.

Wade, A. (1997). Small acts of living: Everyday resistance to violence and other forms of oppression. *Contemporary Family Therapy, 19,* 23–39. doi:10.1023/A:1026154215299

Waldegrave, C. (1996). *Beyond impoverishing treatments of persons.* Keynote speech at the International Narrative Ideas and Therapeutic Practice Conference, Yaletown Family Therapy, Vancouver, British Columbia, Canada.

Waldegrave, C. T. (1990). Just therapy. *Dulwich Centre Newsletter, 1,* 5–46.

Watzlawick, P. (1984). *The invented reality.* New York, NY: Norton.

Weber, M., Davis, K., & McPhie, L. (2006). *Australian Social Work, 59,* 391–405.

Winslade, J., & Monk, G. (2007). *Narrative counseling in schools.* New York, NY: Norton.

White, M. (1979). Structural and strategic approaches to psychodynamic families. *Family Process, 18,* 303–314. doi:10.1111/j.1545-5300.1979.00303.x

White, M. (1984). Pseudo-encopresis: From avalanche to victory, from vicious to virtuous cycles. *Family Systems Medicine, 2,* 150–160. doi:10.1037/h0091651

White, M. (1986). Anorexia nervosa: A cybernetic perspective. In J. Elka-Harkaway (Ed.), *Eating disorders and family therapy* (pp. 67–73). New York, NY: Aspen.

White, M. (1987). Family therapy and schizophrenia: Addressing the "in-the-corner" lifestyle. *Dulwich Centre Newsletter* (spring), 14–21.

White, M. (1988). *Selected papers.* Adelaide, South Australia: Dulwich Centre Publications.

White, M. (1988/1989). *The externalizing of the problem and the re-authoring of lives and relationships. Dulwich Centre Newsletter* [Special issue], *Summer,* 3–20.

White, M. (1991). Deconstruction and therapy. In D. Epston & M. White (Eds.), *Experience, contradiction, narrative, and imagination: Selected papers of David Epston and Michael White, 1989–1991.* Adelaide, South Australia: Dulwich Centre Publications.

White, M. (1995a). Psychotic experience and discourse. In M. White (Ed.), *Re-authoring lives: Interviews and essays* (pp. 45–51). Adelaide, South Australia: Dulwich Centre Publications.

White, M. (1995b). Reflecting teamwork as definitional ceremony. In M. White (Ed.), *Re-authoring lives: Interviews and essays* (pp. 16–26). Adelaide, South Australia: Dulwich Centre Publications.

White, M. (1997). *Narratives of therapists' lives.* Adelaide, South Australia: Dulwich Centre Publications.

White, M. (1999). Reflecting teamwork as definitional ceremony revisited. *Gecko: A journal of deconstruction and narrative ideas in therapeutic practice, 1,* 55–82.

White, M. (2002). Addressing personal failure. *International Journal of Narrative Therapy and Community Work, 3,* 33–76.

White, M. (2004). *Narrative practice and exotic lives: Resurrecting diversity in everyday life.* Adelaide, South Australia: Dulwich Centre Publications.

White, M. (2005). Children, trauma and subordinate storyline development. *The International Journal of Narrative Therapy and Community Work, 3/4,* 10–22.

White, M. (2007). *Maps of narrative practice.* New York, NY: Norton.

White, M., & Epston, D. (1990). *Narrative means to therapeutic ends.* New York, NY: Norton.

Winslade, J. (2009). Tracing lines of flight: Implications of the work of Gilles Deleuze for narrative practice. *Family Process, 48,* 332–346. doi:10.1111/j.1545-5300.2009.01286.x

Winslade, J., Crocket, K., Epston, D., & Monk, G. (1996). *Narrative therapy practice: The archeology of hope.* San Francisco, CA: Jossey-Bass.

Wittgenstein, L. (1953). *Philosophical investigations* (D. E. Linge, Trans.). Berkeley: University of California Press.

Wittgenstein, L. (1960). *The blue and brown books.* New York, NY: Harper & Row.

Zur, O., & Nordmarken, N. (2007). *DSM: Diagnosing for money and power: Summary of the critique of the DSM.* Sonoma, CA: Zur Institute. Retrieved from http://www.zurinstitute.com/dsmcritique.html

# Index

# About the Author

**Stephen Madigan** holds an MSW and an MSc and PhD in couple and family therapy. In 1992, he opened the Vancouver School for Narrative Therapy through Yaletown Family Therapy in Vancouver, Canada, as the first narrative therapy training site in the Northern Hemisphere. He hosts the yearly Therapeutic Conversations Conference, publishes widely, and teaches narrative training workshops worldwide. In June 2007, the American Family Therapy Academy honored Dr. Madigan with their Distinguished Award for Innovative Practice in Family Therapy Theory and Practice. Dr. Madigan is also a "retired" member of Canada's National Ultimate Frisbee Team. Find out more at http://www.stephenmadigan.ca

# About the Series Editors

**Jon Carlson, PsyD, EdD, ABPP,** is distinguished professor of psychology and counseling at Governors State University in University Park, Illinois, and a psychologist at the Wellness Clinic in Lake Geneva, Wisconsin. Dr. Carlson has served as the editor of several periodicals including the *Journal of Individual Psychology* and *The Family Journal*. He holds diplomates in both family psychology and Adlerian psychology. He has authored 150 journal articles and 40 books, including *Time for a Better Marriage, Adlerian Therapy, The Mummy at the Dining Room Table, Bad Therapy, The Client Who Changed Me,* and *Moved by the Spirit*. He has created more than 200 professional trade video and DVDs with leading professional therapists and educators. In 2004 the American Counseling Association named him a "Living Legend." Recently he syndicated an advice cartoon *On The Edge* with cartoonist Joe Martin.

**Matt Englar-Carlson, PhD,** is an associate professor of counseling at California State University, Fullerton, and an adjunct senior lecturer in the School of Health at the University of New England in Armidale, Australia. He is a fellow of Division 51 of the American Psychological Association (APA). As a scholar, teacher, and clinician, Dr. Englar-Carlson has been an innovator and professionally passionate about training and teaching clinicians to work more effectively with their male clients. He has more than 30 publications and 50 national and international presentations, most of which are focused on men and masculinity. Dr. Englar-Carlson coedited the books *In the Room With Men: A Casebook of Therapeutic Change* and *Counseling Troubled Boys: A Guidebook for Professionals.* In 2007 he was named the Researcher of the Year by the Society for the Psychological Study of Men and Masculinity. He is also a member of the APA Working Group to Develop Guidelines for Psychological Practice With Boys and Men. As a clinician, he has worked with children, adults, and families in school, community, and university mental health settings.